THE TAIWANESE TABLE

The Taiwanese Table

Food from the Isle of Formosa

Jade and Muriel Chen

dragon
TAIWANESE DINING

BLUE EYE DRAGON
NO. 37
PYRMONT STREET

Contents

Dedication

In 2007, when Fiona from New Holland Publishers approached Mum and me with the idea of a cookbook, we weren't sure there would be public interest in Taiwanese cuisine and our personal story. Today, two books and two decades later, it is humbling to know that people appreciate authentic food rooted in culture, family, passion and no-fuss offerings. Fiona, whom I now call 'Fi,' has become a cherished friend, and I thank her for her unwavering support and belief in Mum and me. Publishing this book in time for Blue Eye Dragon's 20-Year celebration was only possible thanks to the generousities of Audra Eng and Joseph Thoennes, Sarah Wang, and Roy Chen. Your support is forever appreciated. To this day, in her 70s, Mum still hasn't let me cook her a proper Taiwanese dinner as she always says, "it's faster I cook, and you don't dirty your clothes". So, this book, *The Taiwanese Table – Food from the Isle of Formosa* is not just a celebration of Taiwanese food – it is a story of a mother's love. A woman who gave everything for her family, one meal at a time.

To my mum, Jade, thank you for everything. This book is for you.

Love, Muriel

Introduction

What is Taiwanese Food? Is Taiwanese food the same as Chinese Food? Yes and no. Is there a clear difference between the two? Yes and no. The close connection between the two dates back centuries. As time moves on, food evolves, as does everything else.

Taiwanese food is shaped by the island's history, geographical location, colonisation, mixed cultural influence and, most importantly, the grit and creativity of small businesses. Native Taiwanese, provincial Chinese and Japanese cuisine can all be seen on the island today, but with innovation and adaptation. With advanced agriculture techniques and located in a sub-tropical zone, Taiwan produces top quality ingredients, abundant varieties of fruits and vegetables, as well as rice, wheat, corn and tea.

In the 16th century, Portuguese sailors called Taiwan 'Ilha Formosa', a 'beautiful island', and the name 'Formosa' is still used today even though the Portuguese never colonised Taiwan. After involuntarily exiting the United Nations in 1972, Taiwanese people had to work harder, be creative and constantly re-invent themselves to survive and thrive on the world stage. This trait is evident in the cuisine.

Street food culture is vibrant in Taiwan, and the small food vendors are the backbone of Taiwan's miracle economy. Indigenous food, Chinese regional cuisine, especially those of the Hakka and Hokkien from the Southeastern Region, as well as Japan's 50 years occupation of Taiwan in the early 20th Century have all blended harmoniously in today's Taiwanese Food.

Food offering in Taiwan has many styles, from night markets, roadside food stalls, hot pot, traditional buffet that you can choose but not self-serve and are charged by weight, to family-run restaurants, cafés, speciality fine dining to high-end multi cuisine buffets. When visiting the night market, you are spoilt for choice as you will find dishes from stir fried, deep fried, grilled, noodles, soups and dumplings to sweets and snacks.

Today, internationally, there are many dishes known as Taiwanese speciality, Salty Crispy Chicken Bites, Oyster Omelette, Oyster Noodle, Minced Pork Rice, Fan-Tuan, Beef Noodles Soup, Gua-Bao, Egg Rolls, Railway Bento Box, Pineapple Cake, Bubble

Tea, Shaved Ice, etc. Generally, Taiwanese food is about comfort, convenience, balance of flavours, creativity and the joy of sharing good food with loved ones.

Recipes in this book are the dishes I remember and love eating whilst growing up and are now served at Blue Eye Dragon, with many dishes only served at staff's meals. These recipes only represent a fraction of the beautiful Taiwanese food and flavour, I hope they will become your favourite to cook and enjoy with families and friends.

My journey of food and 20 Years of Blue Eye Dragon

I wanted to open a restaurant since my university days; the desire was fuelled by the responsibility of cooking for my brother and cousin while Mum travelled between Taiwan and Australia. Since I was exposed to quality food from a very young age, I was quite fussy and picky with my food, and take away was not appealing to me. Neither was always being in the kitchen. I soon realised the best way to get out of cooking was to open a restaurant and have someone else cook everything I loved.

When I started primary school, my parents – Jade and John, sent me to live with my late maternal grandma Liu-Mei because they worked long hours, managing a driving school, running their first Japanese/Taiwanese seafood restaurant, both in Chungli, a small industrial city 40 minutes from Taipei. Some of my earliest memories of delicious food was from those years living with grandma, who had rice fields, vegetable patches, a fishpond, a chicken coop, and even a pig pen. I was surrounded by fresh, seasonal ingredients. To this day, I still remember the taste of food grandma made for me. As a seven-year-old little girl, she was a magician with food, everything was delicious. When I was nine years old, I would hop on a bus on the weekend, travel 30 minutes to see my parents, and they would let me order anything from the fresh display of seafood. It was better than a buffet, not only did I get to choose what I liked, the chef would cook it for me the way I loved to eat it. Those weekend bus trips continued until Mum opened her second restaurant, and my brother and I moved back to the city to live with them.

In junior high school years, when all other students ate lunch boxes reheated in the big communal steamer, I was eating freshly packed lunch boxes. My cousin Christopher, now in heaven watching over me, would hop on his scooter delivering the restaurant cooked lunch box to me daily. The days when Christopher couldn't deliver for me, Aunty Michelle who worked at the school would escort me out to the roadside store for lunch. Spoilt? That is an understatement.

Most evenings, I dined at Mum's restaurant and Mum began teaching me the fundamental cooking skills by telling me if any dish that I had was not perfect. She would focus on the reasons which could be the quality of ingredients, improper preparation, or less than perfect cooking techniques. Rather than providing recipes, she taught me the reasons and principles behind the methods.

Mum learnt her craft by trial and error and from grandma. She started cooking for my uncles and aunties when she was just 13 years old and, decades later, Mum can serve a ten-course dinner for 20 people, for special occasions like birthday or Chinese New Year, without any help or looking at a recipe.

There were a few years when Mum had two restaurants, 400-seat and 1000-seat capacities. She frequently travelled on her motorised scooter between them to ensure a smooth operation of the kitchen during service hours. In Taiwan, Mum rarely had to cook, but this changed when our family migrated to Melbourne in 1989. In the initial years, Mum cooked daily and hosted dinner parties every week, especially for other migrant families. This period marked the beginning of my practical cooking education, particularly as Mum travelled often which meant I had to assume the responsibility of cooking for my younger brother and cousin. Despite my lack of actual experience, Mum's guidance over the years proved invaluable, making the task of cooking less daunting. As Mum always says, cooking is not about recipes – it is about understanding ingredients, relying on sensory to bring out the flavours harmoniously.

While working in Sydney for hotels and tech company in the late 1990s, I craved for the honest, home-style Taiwanese food, not the street snacks or trendy reinventions. For a while, my then boyfriend now husband, David couldn't understand what I was complaining about as he had never had my mum's cooking. I wanted the food that Mum made for us growing up and the food mum's restaurant served in Taiwan. So, one day in 2001, I said to Mum, "I want to open a restaurant, can you help me please?" Without hesitation, Mum said yes. So, after years of delay, in September 2005, Blue Eye Dragon opened on the ground floor of the old Pyrmont Arms Hotel, and that little restaurant became something more than we would ever have imagined.

In 2010, Blue Eye Dragon relocated to our current location, the beautiful heritage St Bede's Hall, also in Pyrmont. We kept everything simple to retain as much character of the building as possible. Despite changing location, our culinary offering and purpose remained, we continued to serve the foods we enjoyed at home, the recipes honed by Mum over the years. Our menu focuses on flavour, balance, freshness, and staying true to a standard that ensures the quality is exactly what we serve at our own table.

Managing Blue Eye Dragon is mostly joy but not without tears. There are moments of fatigue and stress but are always quickly replaced by happiness when I am greeted

by customers with genuine care of how I am doing, seeing three generations of diners celebrating family milestones year after year, regulars bringing their families and friends from near and far to showcase our food, and getting hugs from little ones.

I know Blue Eye Dragon would not have be what it is today, or even exist, without our dedicated staff, loyal customers, supportive suppliers, understanding landlord, and my family. Amanda, Chris, Yen-Fen, Sugi, Anita, Daniel, Michael and Ken always have my back, multitasking to provide the best service and experience for our customers. My husband, David, my children Marcus, Xavier, Lucius and Odin on call to help at any time. I will always remember the day before the COVID lockdown in March 2020, so many customers just showed up to support us by ordering more than they needed.

Special thanks to my friends, Mike and Sally, Sarah, Debby, Christine, Paul, Mei, Sandy, Tony, Peter and Helen, your support means the world to me. To Father Dom and Father James, thank you for the prayers and your faith in me!

Here's to 20 years of Blue Eye Dragon, and to many more shared meals ahead. I extend my gratitude to you for being part of my journey in food.

Basics

In today's modern, busy life we work longer hours and have less time for everything else. If you follow the basics in this section, cooking a meal for four people in 30 minutes will be easy. After each grocery shopping trip, Mum always takes the time to clean, cut and marinate everything, and only then stores them in the fridge or freezer. This way she can cook a meal for the family in a very short time. With this preparation done first, most of the marinating steps in this book will not be required.

Serving sizes

Most of the small and large sharing plate recipes in this book are designed for two people to share over two dishes. If you are cooking for more than two people, instead of doubling on the quantity, maybe just cook another dish.

Mum always asks, 'How many people for dinner?', then she will always cook an extra dish. For example, for four people, she will always make five dishes.

Marinating

Marinating should be very simple and easy, as you do not want to mask the natural flavours of the produce. One thing that is very important to us at Blue Eye Dragon is the freshness and clean-cut taste of the food. Storing the meat or seafood in serving quantity portions of around 250 g (8 oz) makes preparation quicker and less messy. For quick defrosting, pack each portion flat.

Monosodium Glutamate (MSG)

Monosodium is widely used as a flavour enhancer and is naturally found in many foods like cheese and tomatoes. It is commonly added to foods to boost umami taste. It is generally recognized as safe, though some people report mild sensitivity symptoms, but controlled studies have not confirmed a clear link. If you'd like to use MSG for marinating, then there will be no need to use sugar. A tiny pinch will enhance the flavour significantly.

Chicken and Pork

Whether it is chicken thigh or breast fillet, it is important to trim away the fat before cooking because this makes a difference to the taste. With chicken, unlike beef or pork, you need to cut along the grain.

Pork is a beautiful pink meat that the Asians love. Pork cheek is the best for stir frying texture wise, but it is difficult to get. If you are concerned about fat, lean pork or pork loin are good. Pork is tougher than chicken so thinly slice against the grain.

To marinate 1 kg (2 lb) of chicken or pork:

½ teaspoon salt
1 teaspoon sugar
1 egg white, beaten
2 tablespoons potato flour (see ***Glossary***)
60 ml (2 fl oz) water
2 tablespoons vegetable oil

- Mix all the ingredients except the oil together using a lifting motion with your hands, until you can feel the water has been absorbed by the meat.
- Add the vegetable oil and mix well.
- Freeze in airtight containers in desired serving portions, 250 g (8 oz) is suggested throughout this book.

Beef

Beef skirt steak or flank steak is best for stir frying. It is a more expensive cut, but it is worth the money. Make sure you cut against the grain, otherwise it will end up as chewy as beef jerky.

To marinate 1 kg (2 lb) of beef:

1 teaspoon sugar
½ egg, beaten
2 tablespoons potato flour (see ***Glossary***)
1 tablespoon soy sauce
120 ml (4 fl oz) water
2 tablespoons vegetable oil

Note: do not use salt if marinating beef

- Mix all the ingredients except the oil together using a lifting motion with your hands, until you can feel the water has been absorbed by the meat.
- Add the vegetable oil and mix well.
- Freeze in airtight containers in desired serving portions, 250 g (8 oz) is suggested throughout this book.

Prawns (Shrimp)

To preserve freshness, peel and devein the prawns before marinating.

When freezing fresh (not peeled or marinated) prawns, best to freeze them in water.

To marinate 1 kg (2 lb) of peeled prawns:

¼ teaspoon salt
½ teaspoon sugar
1 egg white
3 tablespoons cornflour
ground white pepper, a pinch

- Mix all the ingredients together and add to prawns. Freeze in airtight containers in desired serving portions. 8 prawns are suggested throughout this book.

Fish

Fish fillets should be cleaned and frozen in desired serving portions. If freezing a whole fish, make sure the fish is cleaned and gutted thoroughly. Then freeze in an airtight container.

Storing vegetables

There is an old Chinese saying: 'Money knows quality' meaning that expensive produce is expensive for a reason. Of course, the best vegetables are always those in season.

Vegetables are the trickiest stir-fry ingredients to keep fresh. Mum always purchases the best and spends time washing them and removing any yellow or loose leaves prior to storing them accordingly. She will wrap them in paper towels then in containers. Mum frequently jokes that she treats the vegetables like she treats us; with lots of love and care.

Wok Stir-Fry

The key to great stir frying is always heat the wok before adding oil, and make sure it is very hot before you start cooking. Never stir fry large amounts at once – doing so will stew the ingredients instead of searing them. If you need to make a bigger portion, it is better to cook the dish twice than doubling everything in one stir fry.

Deep Fry

A portable counter top deep fryer is worth the investment as you can set the temperature just by using the dial. If you don't have a deep fryer then heat the oil in a wok. To test if it is at 180°C (350°F), the normal temperature for deep-frying, place a small cube of bread into the hot oil. If it browns within 1 minute, it is hot enough.

Fried Red Shallots

Fried Red Shallots are a staple in many Asian cuisines. Across Southeast Asia, they are sprinkled on salads, fried rice, and soups. In Taiwan, they are essential for pork- or chicken-based noodle soups, hence, the oil used to fried the shallot is always kept. They also add depth to a variety of cooked dishes – and can even work beautifully in pasta sauces.

For extra richness, try frying them in pork lard to enhance their flavour.

2 kg (4 lb) red shallots, skinned and thinly sliced
500 ml (16 fl oz) vegetable oil or pork lard

- Heat a wok over high heat and add the oil.
- Once the oil is hot, add a handful of shallots at a time, stirring continuously.
- After the moisture has evaporated, reduce the heat to medium.
- Keep stirring constantly to prevent the shallots from sticking or burning, as the natural sugars will caramelise.
- When the shallots start to turn golden brown, quickly remove and drain them. Spread them out on a tray to cool – they will continue to brown slightly after coming out of the wok.
- Repeat the process with the remaining shallots. You can reuse the oil throughout, adding more if needed for easier frying.
- Once everything has cooled, mix the fried shallots with the oil.
- Store in an airtight container in the fridge – they'll stay fresh for months.

Sauces

Sauces

Stir frying is all about balancing the natural flavours of each ingredient – too much sauce, and the dish turns into a stew! Salt and sugar are normally enough for a light flavoured dish as the ingredients, blended in a very hot wok, will become surprisingly flavoursome.

Soy sauce is the most used and most important flavour enhancer. Its quality has a big impact on the final taste of the dish.

Here are some ready-made bottled sauces that can be purchased in Asian grocery stores. They are a must for the pantry and are what we use throughout this book.

Kim Ve Wong Soy Sauce
Kim Lan Soy Paste
Kong Yen Black Vinegar
Kong Yen Rice Vinegar
Bull Head Barbecue Sauce
Rice wine

In addition to these sauces, here are the essential ingredients used throughout this book to make stir frying easy and delicious.

five spice powder
ground white pepper
garlic
shallots (spring onions/scallions)
ginger
chilli
coriander (cilantro)
star anise

Dumpling Dipping Sauce

MAKES JUST OVER 100 ML, ENOUGH FOR SEVERAL SERVINGS.

25 ml (¾ fl oz) chilli paste
75 ml (2½ fl oz) soy sauce
1 teaspoon sesame oil
1 tablespoon rice vinegar

- Mix all the ingredients. Store unused sauce in bottles to refrigerate.

Taiwanese Sweet and Sour Sauce

MAKES APPROX 1 CUP

2½ tablespoons sugar
¼ tablespoon black vinegar (see *Glossary*)
½ teaspoon soy sauce
125 ml (4 fl oz) water
1 teaspoon potato flour (see *Glossary*)

- Combine potato flour with 1 teaspoon of water to make a paste.
- Mix all the ingredients in a big pot, bring to the boil and stir in the paste to thicken the sauce.
- Allow to cool before storing in bottles to refrigerate.

Sweet and Sour Sauce

MAKES APPROX 4 CUPS

250 ml (8 fl oz) water
250 ml (8 fl oz) tomato sauce
250 ml (8 fl oz) sugar
250 ml (8 fl oz) rice vinegar (see *Glossary*)
¼ teaspoon preserved Chinese plum powder (optional – see *Glossary*)

- Combine all ingredients and bring to the boil.
- Allow to cool before storing in bottles to refrigerate.

Fish Sauce

MAKES APPROX 2½ CUPS

500 ml (16 fl oz) water
125 ml (4 fl oz) store-bought fish sauce
80 g (2¾ oz) white rock sugar (see *Glossary*)
3 slices dry licorice

- In a pot, bring the water and dry licorice to the boil. Add all ingredients, stir and bring back to the boil. Remove the dry licorice. Allow to cool before storing in bottles to refrigerate.
- This fish sauce is a milder taste, and the licorice takes the flavour to another level.

Jade's Bloody Plum Sauce

MAKES APPROX 4 CUPS

¼ tablespoon preserved Chinese plum powder (see *Glossary*)
125 ml (4 fl oz) rice vinegar (see *Glossary*)
½ tablespoon black vinegar (see *Glossary*)
½ tablespoon Worcestershire sauce
250 ml (8 fl oz) tomato sauce
½ tablespoon HP sauce (steak sauce)
500 ml (16 fl oz) sugar
chilli oil, a drizzle (see *Glossary*)
250 ml (8 fl oz) water

- In a pot, bring water and all ingredients to the boil. Stir constantly.
- Allow to cool before storing in bottles to refrigerate.

Taiwanese Garlic Five Spice Sauce

MAKES APPROX 2 CUPS

250 ml (8 fl oz) tomato sauce
60 ml (2 fl oz) sugar
60 ml (2 fl oz) soy paste (see *Glossary*)
60 ml (2 fl oz) black vinegar (see *Glossary*)
1 teaspoon sesame oil
1 teaspoon chilli oil (see *Glossary*)
2 shallots (spring onions/scallions), finely chopped
10 slices ginger, finely chopped
5 cloves garlic, finely chopped
1 large red chilli, finely chopped or deseeded if required
1 small bunch coriander (cilantro), finely chopped

- Combine tomato sauce, sugar, soy paste, vinegar, sesame oil and chilli oil, then stir until sugar has dissolved.
- Add the shallots, ginger, garlic, chilli and coriander and mix well.

NOTE
This makes a large quantity, and unused sauce can be refrigerated in airtight bottles. This is great over squid, oysters and other seafood or as a barbecue marinade.

Garlic Chilli Sauce with Chilli Beans

MAKES APPROX 5 – 6 CUPS

500 g (1 lb) small hot chillies, finely chopped
300 g (9½ oz) garlic, minced
1 litre (32 fl oz) vegetable oil
60 ml (2 fl oz) sesame oil
150 g (5 oz) chilli bean sauce (see *Glossary*)

- Spread the chillies evenly over a deep, large baking tray then sprinkle the garlic over the chillies.
- Heat oil to 200°C (400°F) in a wok, then turn off the heat.
- Use a large ladle to drizzle the hot oil all over the chillies and garlic, until all the garlic turns golden brown.
- Then stir the chillies and garlic together and continue to pour the hot oil over them.
- Add the chilli beans sauce and sesame oil, then mix thoroughly.
- Allow to cool before storing in bottles to refrigerate.

NOTE
To store the sauce in the fridge, make sure the chillies are fully covered in oil.
If for any reason the oil is consumed faster than the chillies, add more sesame oil to cover.

Caramelised Gong-Bao Sauce

MAKES APPROX 2 CUPS

Part One

125 ml (4 fl oz) sugar
125 ml (4 fl oz) water

Part Two

1 teaspoon ground white pepper
125 ml (4 fl oz) sugar
2 pieces white rock sugar (see *Glossary*)
100 ml (3½ fl oz) soy sauce
125 ml (4 fl oz) black vinegar (see *Glossary*)

1 tablespoon glutinous rice flour (see *Glossary*)

Part One

- Cook the sugar with half of the water in a wok, stirring continuously. The mixture will turn red in colour then dark brown.
- Add the rest of the water and stir well.

Part Two

- Add all Part Two ingredients to part one and bring to the boil.
- Combine the glutinous rice flour with 1 tablespoon of water to make a paste.
- Add the paste to the wok and stir well until sauce thickens.
- Allow to cool before storing in bottles to refrigerate.

Salt and Pepper

Salt and Pepper Mixture

MAKES APPROX 1 CUP

4 tablespoons salt
2 tablespoons sugar
1 tablespoon ground white pepper

- Combine the salt, sugar and pepper in a spice grinder or mortar and pestle and mix until well blended.
- When preparing large quantities, it is best to first wok toss the salt over low heat to remove any excess moisture.

NOTE

Salt and pepper dishes are very popular in Chinese and Taiwanese cuisine.

There are several ways to do it. The process we use at Blue Eye Dragon is simple, but the crucial steps of wok tossing must be done exactly right to get a perfect result!

Left over mixture can be stored in a well-sealed jar in a cool place (not refrigerated) for up to 3 months.

Salt and Pepper Squid

SERVES 2 – 4

1 whole squid
1 tablespoon Salt and Pepper Mixture (see page 38)
vegetable oil, for deep-frying
250 ml (8 fl oz) cornflour
4–5 cloves garlic, finely sliced
1 long chilli, chopped (deseeded if preferred to minimise the spiciness)
2 shallots (spring onions/scallions), green section only, chopped

- Clean the squid, cut the tubes open and cut a crosshatch pattern into the insides. Be careful not to cut all the way through.
- Cut the tubes into 4 x 2 cm (2 x 1 in) pieces and place in a mixing bowl with one pinch of the Salt and Pepper Mixture, mix well.
- Heat the oil in a deep fryer (or wok, see ***Basics***) to 180°C (350°F).
- Place the cornflour in a bowl and slowly add in enough water to make a batter with a consistency that is thicker than paint and slightly sticky.
- Then add in the squid.
- Use your whole hand to mix the squid with the batter, don't just coat the surface.
- Slowly lower the squid into the hot oil, it should float when ready.
- Remove from the oil immediately, drain on paper towels.
- Lightly oil a wok, place over high heat, throw in the garlic for a good stir and then the chilli and shallots.
- Finally add the cooked squid, sprinkle with some of the Salt and Pepper Mixture and give it all a good toss.
- Serve with some of the remaining mixture on the side.

NOTE

Use as little oil as possible when tossing the shallots, garlic and chilli. You don't want any excess oil to be absorbed into the batter. A good trick is to use a spray vegetable oil or rub a paper towel with a little oil on it over the wok.

Salt and Pepper Prawns

SERVES 2 – 4

10 large fresh tiger prawns (shrimp), cleaned, deveined with tail on
1 tablespoon Salt and Pepper Mixture (see page 38)
vegetable oil, for deep-frying
250 g (8 oz) cornflour
4–5 cloves garlic, finely sliced
1 long chilli, chopped (deseeded if preferred to minimise the spiciness)
2 shallots (spring onions/scallions), green section only, chopped

- Place the prawns (shrimp) in a mixing bowl with one pinch of the Salt and Pepper Mixture, mix well.
- Heat the oil in a deep fryer (or wok, see ***Basics***) to 180°C (350°F).
- Put cornflour a bowl and slowly add in enough water to make a batter with a consistency that is thicker than paint and slightly sticky.
- Then add in the prawns.
- Use your whole hand to mix the prawns with the batter, don't just coat the surface.
- Slowly lower the prawns into the hot oil, they should float when ready.
- Remove from the oil immediately, drain on paper towels.
- Lightly oil a wok, turn on high heat, throw in the garlic for a good stir, and then the chilli and shallots.
- Finally add the cooked prawns, sprinkle with some of the Salt and Pepper Mixture and give it all a good toss.
- Serve with the remaining Salt and Pepper Mixture on the side.

NOTE

Use as little oil as possible when tossing the shallots, garlic and chilli. You don't want any excess oil to be absorbed into the batter. A good trick is to use a spray vegetable oil or rub a paper towel with a little oil on it over the wok.

Salt and Pepper Soft Shell Crab

SERVES 2

150 g (5 oz) soft shell crab
1 tablespoon Salt and Pepper Mixture (see page 38)
vegetable oil, for deep-frying
250 g (8 oz) cornflour
4–5 cloves garlic, finely sliced
1 long chilli, chopped (deseeded if preferred to minimise the spiciness)
2 shallots (spring onions/scallions), green section only, chopped

- Clean and cut each crab into 6 pieces.
- Place the crab pieces in a mixing bowl with one pinch of the Salt and Pepper Mixture, mix well.
- Heat the oil in a deep fryer (or wok, see ***Basics***) to 180°C (350°F).
- Put cornflour in the bowl with the crab pieces.
- Coat the crab pieces well, allow to rest for a minute.
- Shake off excess flour before deep-frying.
- Slowly lower the crab pieces into the hot oil, they should float when ready.
- Remove from the oil immediately, drain on paper towels.
- Lightly oil a wok, turn on high heat, throw in the garlic for a good stir, and then the chilli and shallots.
- Finally add the cooked crab, sprinkle with some of the Salt and Pepper Mixture and give it all a good toss.
- Serve with the remaining Salt and Pepper Mixture on the side.

NOTE

Use as little oil as possible when tossing the shallots, garlic and chilli. You don't want any excess oil to be absorbed into the batter. A good trick is to use a spray vegetable oil or rub a paper towel with a little oil on it over the wok.

Salt and Pepper Tofu

SERVES 2 – 4

250 g (8 oz) cornflour
250 g (8 oz) tofu, cut into bite size pieces
vegetable oil, for deep-frying
4–5 cloves garlic, finely sliced
1 long chilli, chopped (deseeded if preferred to minimise the spiciness)
2 shallots (spring onions/scallions), green section only, chopped
½ tablespoon Salt and Pepper Mixture (see page 38)

- Heat the oil in a deep fryer (or wok, see ***Basics***) to 180°C (350°F).
- Put cornflour in a bowl and add the tofu. Gently coat the tofu and allow to rest for a minute.
- Deep-fry until golden brown.
- Remove from the oil immediately, drain on paper towels.
- Lightly oil a wok, turn on high heat, throw in the garlic for a good stir, then the chilli and shallots.
- Finally add the cooked tofu, sprinkle with some of the Salt and Pepper Mixture and give it all a good toss.
- Serve with the remaining Salt and Pepper Mixture on the side.

NOTE

Use as little oil as possible when tossing the shallots, garlic and chilli. You don't want any excess oil to be absorbed into the batter. A good trick is to use a spray vegetable oil or rub a paper towel with a little oil on it over the wok.

Salt and Pepper Whitebait

SERVES 2 – 4

200 g (6½ oz) whitebait
1 tablespoon Salt and Pepper Mixture (see page 38)
vegetable oil, for deep-frying
125 g (4 oz) cornflour
4–5 cloves garlic, finely sliced
1 long chilli, chopped (deseeded if preferred to minimise the spiciness)
2 shallots (spring onions/scallions), green section only, chopped

- Wash and drain the whitebait well. Mix the whitebait with the cornflour in a mixing bowl.
- Remove the whitebait and shake off excess flour.
- Heat the oil in a deep fryer (or wok, see ***Basics***) to 180°C (350°F).
- Deep-fry the whitebait until golden brown.
- Remove from the oil immediately, drain on paper towels.
- Lightly oil a wok, turn on high heat, throw in the garlic for a good stir, then the chilli and shallots.
- Finally add the cooked whitebait, sprinkle with some of the Salt and Pepper Mixture and give it all a good toss.
- Serve with the remaining Salt and Pepper Mixture on the side.

NOTE

Use as little oil as possible when tossing the shallots, garlic and chilli. You don't want any excess oil to be absorbed into the batter. A good trick is to use a spray vegetable oil or rub a paper towel with a little oil on it over the wok.

Salt and Pepper Fish Fillets

SERVES 2

200 g (6½ oz) basa fish fillet, cut to 2.5 cm (1 in) wide strips
2 tablespoons plain flour
a pinch salt
a pinch sugar
2 teaspoons Salt and Pepper Mixture (see page 38)
250 g (8 oz) cornflour
vegetable oil, for frying

- Heat the oil in a deep fryer (or wok, see ***Basics***) to 180°C (350°F).
- In a bowl, marinate the fish pieces with salt and sugar, then set aside.
- Mix the plain flour with some water to form a lumpy consistency.
- Place the marinated fish pieces in the flour mixture and coat well.
- On a tray, dust the fish pieces with cornflour and let it rest for few seconds.
- Deep-fry the fish until golden brown.
- Remove from the oil immediately, drain on paper towels.
- Sprinkle the Salt and Pepper Mixture on the fish fillet, plate up.
- Serve with remaining Salt and Pepper Mixture on the side.

Small Sharing Plates

Deep-Fried Crumbed Chicken Fillets

SERVES 2

250 g (8 oz) chicken breast fillets
2 teaspoons Salt and Pepper Mixture (see page 38)
½ teaspoon curry powder
2 eggs, lightly beaten
500 g (16 oz) cornflour
500 g (16 oz) breadcrumbs
vegetable oil, for deep-frying
coriander (cilantro), finely chopped for serving

- Trim each fillet into palm-sized pieces, making sure they are all the same thickness to ensure even cooking.
- Marinate the chicken with a pinch of the Salt and Pepper Mixture, curry powder and ½ tablespoon of the lightly beaten egg and allow to rest for about 5 minutes.
- Heat the oil in a deep fryer (or wok, see ***Basics***) to 180°C (350°F).
- On both sides, lightly dust the chicken fillets with the cornflour and then coat with the remaining beaten egg, before covering evenly with breadcrumbs.
- Allow to stand for about a minute before deep-frying.
- Once the chicken starts to float and turn golden brown, they are cooked.
- Drain them on paper towels to absorb excess oil.
- Cut the chicken fillets into long strips, sprinkle with coriander (cilantro).
- Serve with the remaining Salt and Pepper Mixture on the side.

Crispy Chicken with Basil and Five Spice

SERVES 2

3 teaspoons Salt and Pepper Mixture (see page 38)
½ teaspoon five spice powder (see *Glossary*)
salt, pinch
sugar, pinch
250 g (8 oz) chicken fillet, cut into 2 x 1 cm (¾ x ½ in) pieces
250 g (8 oz) cornflour or sweet potato flour (see *Glossary*)
125 g (4 oz) basil leaves
vegetable oil, for deep-frying

- Combine the salt and pepper mix with the five-spice powder in a spice grinder or mortar until well blended. Set aside.
- Marinate the chicken with a pinch of cornflour, salt, and sugar, and let it stand for a few minutes.
- Heat oil in a deep fryer (or wok, see ***Basics***) to 180°C (350°F).
- Lightly dust the chicken pieces with the remaining cornflour and rest for a minute before frying.
- Fry the chicken until the pieces float and turn golden brown. Drain on paper towels.
- Before frying the basil, have a lid ready – the leaves will cause the oil to splatter. Fry for 1 minute until crisp, then drain on paper towels.
- In a large bowl, toss the chicken with the fried basil and sprinkle with some of the salt, pepper, and five spice mixture.
- To serve, place the chicken on a plate, top with the basil, and serve the remaining spice mix on the side.

Crispy Chicken Wings

SERVES 4

Marinade

2 cloves garlic, minced
1 teaspoon salt
1 teaspoon sugar
1 teaspoon curry powder
½ egg, lightly beaten
a pinch, ground white pepper
2 tablespoons cornflour
1 kg (2 lb) chicken wings (about 12 wings, mid-section only)
500 g (1 lb) sweet potato flour (preferably crumbed – see *Glossary*)
1 tablespoon Salt and Pepper Mixture (see page 38)
vegetable oil, for deep-frying

- Combine the marinade ingredients and rub onto the chicken wings.
- Heat the oil in a deep fryer (or wok, see ***Basics***) to 180°C (350°F).
- Coat the wings with the sweet potato flour, making sure they are well covered.
- Allow to rest for about 1 minute.
- Shake off any excess flour and place the wings in the deep fryer.
- Once the wings starts to float and turn golden brown, they are cooked. Drain on paper towels to remove excess oil.
- Sprinkle some of the Salt and Pepper Mixture evenly over the chicken.
- Serve with the remaining Salt and Pepper Mixture on the side.

Spicy Chicken Wings Caramelised in Soy Sauce

SERVES 4

1 kg (2 lb) chicken wings (10–12 wings), mid-section
5 garlic cloves, crushed, skin on
1 small red chilli, chopped (deseeded if preferred to minimise the spiciness)
1 shallot (spring onions/scallions), cleaned, whole
½ teaspoon sugar
60 ml (2 fl oz) soy sauce
125 ml (4 fl oz) water

To serve
sesame oil, to drizzle
cucumber slices, to garnish

- Add all the ingredients in a wok and bring to the boil.
- Simmer for 15 minutes and stir constantly.
- When cooked, turn on high heat and continue stirring to reduce the sauce to caramelise.
- Drizzle with sesame oil and serve with cucumber slices.

NOTE

This dish tastes just as good when it is cool.

You can also barbecue the cooked wings for a different taste, great for picnics in the summer.

Tea-Smoked Chicken

SERVES 4

1 kg (2 lb) Chicken Maryland
2 litres (3½ pints) water
60 g (2 oz) ginger, sliced
2 shallots (spring onions/scallions)
½ tablespoon sugar
125 ml (4 fl oz) tea
1 tablespoon salt
Soy and chilli sauce to serve.

- Bring the water to the boil in a big pot.
- Add ginger, shallots, salt and Chicken Maryland.
- Bring back to the boil, then simmer for 15 minutes. Remove and drain Marylands.
- Line a wok with foil.
- Spread the tea and sugar across the foil and place the Marylands on a mesh stand in the wok over the foil.
- Turn on medium heat and cover with a lid to smoke the chicken. When the 'yellow' smoke can be seen evaporates out of the edge of the lid, turn off the heat and let it rest for 2–3 minutes, before you open the lid.
- The colour should be light brown. When the Marylands cool down the colour will darken.
- Cut the Marylands in pieces to serve, with chilli and soy sauce on the side.

NOTE

Traditionally, in Taiwan, we smoke the whole chicken.

This recipe can be used with any part of the chicken or the whole chicken, with the skin on.

Chilli Chicken Wontons

SERVES 4 – 6

Filling

250 g (8 oz) minced chicken
salt, ground white pepper, sugar, a pinch
2 teaspoons potato flour (see *Glossary*)
1 tablespoon water

Sauces

1 teaspoon Garlic Chilli Sauce with Chilli Beans (see *Sauces*)
2 tablespoons Dumpling Sauce for Dumplings (see *Sauces*)

coriander (cilantro), to serve
1 packet huntun (wonton) pastry (see *Glossary*)
¼ lettuce, shredded, to serve

- Mix all the filling ingredients together until the water is absorbed into the chicken.
- Place one teaspoon of chicken mince in the centre of a wonton pastry.
- Spread the mixture out over two-thirds of the pastry.
- Spreading out the filling means a pocket of air is left inside the pastry which makes them float.
- Gather the edges of the pastry at the top. Pinch and twist to seal the top lightly.
- Repeat with the rest of the pastry and mince.
- Bring a large pot of water to the boil.
- Place the wontons in the boiling water, stirring occasionally to avoid them from sticking to the pot.
- Once they float to the surface, wait a further two minutes, then drain them and put into a mixing bowl.
- Stir in the sauces then serve the wontons over the shredded lettuce.
- Garnish with coriander to serve.

Prawn Spring Rolls

MAKES 25 – 30 SPRING ROLLS DEPENDING ON FILLING SIZE

Filling

160 g (5 oz) water chestnuts, diced
¼ teaspoon salt
¼ teaspoon sugar
1 tablespoon potato flour (see *Glossary*)
½ tablespoon bonito powder (see *Glossary*)
600 g (1¼ lb) prawns (shrimp), peeled, deveined and diced
100 g (4 oz) yellow chives, cut into 2 cm (¾ in) pieces (see *Glossary*)
30 g (1 oz) shallots (spring onions/ scallions), finely chopped

1 tablespoon plain flour
30 sheets spring roll pastry (10 cm / 4 in size) (see *Glossary*)
1 piece nori paper, cut into approximate ½ cm (¼ in) x 10 cm (4 in) strips
vegetable oil – for frying
2 tablespoons Plum Sauce (see *Sauces*)

- Mix well all the filling ingredients except for the yellow chives and shallots.
- Then add the yellow chives and shallots and mix again.
- Mix the plain flour with 1 tablespoon of water to make a paste.
- Fill a spring roll pastry with a tablespoon of the mixture.
- Spread the mixture evenly over half of the pastry. Roll it up and seal with the flour paste.
- Wrap a strip of nori around the centre of each roll, secure with flour paste.
- Repeat with the remaining pastry and filling.
- Heat the oil in a deep fryer (or wok, see ***Basics***) to 180°C (350°F).
- Fry the rolls until they start to float and are lightly brown.
- Drain on paper towels to remove excess oil.
- Serve with some plum sauce on the side.

Deep-Fried Prawns with Plum Sauce

SERVES 3 – 4

Salt and Pepper Mixture, a pinch (see page 38)
250 g (8 oz) cornflour
10 tiger prawns (shrimp), peeled, deveined, tail left on
vegetable oil
2 tablespoons plum sauce (see *Sauces*)

- Mix the Salt and Pepper Mixture and 1 tablespoon of cornflour.
- Combine with the prawns (shrimp) and leave to marinate.
- Heat the oil in a deep fryer (or wok, see ***Basics***) to 180°C (350°F).
- Coat the prawns with the remaining cornflour in a tray.
- Let the prawns rest for about a minute before deep-frying.
- Prawns are cooked when curled and floating.
- Remove the prawns.
- Drain on paper towels to absorb excess oil before serving on a plate with the plum sauce.

NOTE
If plum sauce is not available, use sweet chilli sauce or Salt and Pepper Mixture.

Calamari Salad with Taiwanese Garlic Five Spice Sauce

SERVES 1

150 g (5 oz) calamari, cleaned, cross cut from inside in bite size pieces
2 large lettuce leaves, cut into large chunks
3 tablespoons Taiwanese Garlic Five Spice Sauce (see Sauces)

- Bring water in a medium pot to boil, then add in the calamari to blanch quickly, for no more than 20 seconds. Remove calamari and drain well.
- Serve the calamari on a bed of lettuce or mixed leaf salad. Pour the sauce over the top of the calamari to serve.

NOTE

The cutting of calamari has to be done from inside for the calamari to curl up.

Calamari can be replaced with squid.

Scallops with Shallots and Fish Sauce

SERVES 2 – 4

60 ml (2 fl oz) Fish Sauce (see *Sauces*)
12 scallops, cleaned, roe on or off depending on personal preference
1 shallot (spring onion/scallion), finely julienned, then washed, spun dry and drained on paper towels
2 slices carrot, finely julienned

- Mix shallots and carrots together.
- Heat up the fish sauce and keep warm.
- Bring some water to the boil in a pot.
- Place the scallops gently in the water and cook for about one minute, or when colour changes to white.
- Quickly remove them from the pot and onto a serving plate.
- Top scallops with shallots and carrots, then spoon the fish sauce over each one.
- Serve.

Vegetarian Spring Rolls

MAKES 20 – 25 SPRING ROLLS DEPENDANT ON FILLING SIZE

400 g (13 oz) cabbage, shredded
125 g (4 oz) carrots, shredded
250 g (8 oz) celery, shredded
2 tablespoons vegetable oil
½ teaspoon salt
½ teaspoon sugar
¼ teaspoon ground white pepper
3 tablespoons potato flour (see *Glossary*)
1 tablespoon plain flour
2 tablespoons Plum Sauce (see *Sauces*)
25 sheets spring roll pastry (10 cm / 4 in size) (see *Glossary*)

- Mix cabbage, carrots and celery together. In a big pot of boiling water, add vegetable oil, quickly blanch the vegetables for few seconds, remove and drain well. Use a spinner if available.
- In a big bowl, mix salt, sugar and pepper with the vegetables, then gradually add in the potato flour and mix well.
- Mix the plain flour with 1 tablespoon of water to make a paste.
- Fill a spring roll pastry with 2 tablespoons of the mixture.
- Spread the mixture evenly over half of the pastry. Roll it up and seal with the flour paste.
- Repeat with the remaining pastry and filling.
- Heat the oil in a deep fryer (or wok, see ***Basics***) to 180°C (350°F).
- Fry the rolls until they start to float and are lightly brown.
- Drain on paper towels to remove excess oil.
- Serve with plum sauce on the side.

NOTE

Do not roll the spring rolls too tightly or they will burst while deep-frying.

You can freeze the spring rolls in an airtight container. For a faster deep-fry of frozen spring rolls, microwave each roll for about 15 seconds.

Lettuce Wraps with Prawns

MAKES 4

60 g (2 oz) pine nuts
125 g (4 oz) celery, chopped
125 g (4 oz) water chestnuts, chopped
125 g (4 oz) bamboo shoots, chopped
1 tablespoon carrot, chopped
8 large tiger prawns (shrimp), peeled, deveined and chopped
60 ml (2 oz) vegetable oil
1 teaspoon Salt and Pepper Mixture (see page 38)
1 shallot (spring onion/scallion), chopped
4 iceberg lettuce leaves, trimmed to rice bowl-sized cups
sesame oil, drizzle

- Toast pine nuts by stirring them in a dry frying pan over medium heat for a few minutes, until they start to colour – watch them closely as they burn easily.
- Bring a large saucepan of water to the boil, add celery, water chestnuts, bamboo shoots and carrots for a minute. Drain very well, set aside.
- Heat the oil in a wok over high heat, stir fry the prawns (shrimp) for about one to two minutes, then add the vegetables and Salt and Pepper Mixture for further stir and then add the drizzle of sesame oil.
- Stir in shallots and remove from heat.
- Spoon the mixture into lettuce cups, sprinkle with pine nuts and serve.

Prawn Dumplings

MAKES 30 – 40 DUMPLINGS DEPENDING ON FILLING SIZE

Filling

500 g (1 lbs) prawns (shrimp), peeled, deveined and diced
25 g (1 oz) Chinese celery, chopped finely (see *Glossary*)
75 g (2½ oz) shallots (spring onions/scallions), chopped finely
150 g (9 oz) water chestnuts (canned), diced
½ teaspoon ground white pepper
25 g (1 oz) potato flour (see *Glossary*)

1 bag dumpling wrappers, 30–40 pieces (see *Glossary*)
dipping sauce for dumplings (see *Sauces*)

- Mix all the filling ingredients together, then stir in the potato flour until well combined.
- Place 1 tablespoon of the filling in the centre of a piece of wrapper, dab around the edges with water.
- Fold the wrapper together by pressing on the top edge of the wrapper first and then pleat the sides together to shape the dumpling.
- Bring a large pot of water to a boil. Add the dumplings, stirring gently to prevent sticking. Once the water returns to a boil, reduce the heat slightly. Dumplings should start to float after 5 minutes.
- Wait for another minute before removing them from the pot.
- Serve with dipping sauce.
- To pan-fry: Place boiled dumplings on a lightly oiled non-stick pan first before turning on the heat. Fry until the bottoms are golden and crispy.

NOTE

Fresh dumplings need to be left in the freezer on a tray, to shape and harden before being packed in a container to freeze.

Dumplings can be kept in the freezer for up to 2 months and take 8–10 minutes to cook.

Pork Dumplings

MAKES 30 – 40 DEPENDING ON FILLING SIZE

Seasoning

½ teaspoon salt
¾ teaspoon sugar
¾ teaspoon ground white pepper
1½ teaspoons ginger, minced
½ teaspoon soy sauce
80 ml (2½ fl oz) water

1 bag dumpling wrappers, 30–40 pieces (see *Glossary*)
dipping sauce for dumplings (see *Sauces*)

Filling

500 g (1 lb) minced (ground) pork
150 g (5 oz) garlic chives, finely chopped
1 shallot (spring onions/scallions), green section only, finely chopped
2½ tablespoons potato flour (see *Glossary*)
sesame oil, a drizzle

- Mix all the seasoning ingredients together until fully dissolved.
- Add the seasoning mixture to the pork mince. Using your hands, gradually mix in one direction until the seasoning is completely absorbed.
- In a separate bowl, combine the chives, shallots, and potato flour. Add this mixture to the pork mince and mix thoroughly. Finally, add the sesame oil and mix again until well combined.
- Place 1 tablespoon of the filling in the centre of a piece of wrapper, dab around the edges with water.
- Fold the wrapper together by pressing on the top edge of the wrapper first and then pleat the sides together to shape the dumpling.
- Bring a large pot of water to a boil. Add the dumplings, stirring gently to prevent sticking. Once the water returns to a boil, reduce the heat slightly. Dumplings should start to float after 6 minutes.
- Wait for another 2 minutes before removing them from the pot.
- Serve with dipping sauce.
- To pan-fry: Place boiled dumplings on a lightly oiled nonstick pan first before turning on the heat. Fry until the bottoms are golden and crispy.

NOTE

Fresh dumplings need to be left in the freezer on a tray, to shape and harden before being packed in a container to freeze.

Dumplings can be kept in the freezer for up to 2 months and take 10–12 minutes to cook.

Chicken Roll with Water Chestnuts and Hundred Spices

MAKES 4 ROLLS

Dry Ingredients

1 teaspoon ground white pepper
2 tablespoons potato flour (see *Glossary*)
250 g (8 oz) onion, diced
200 ml (7 fl oz) water chestnuts (canned), diced
1 teaspoon Bai-Chao (Hundred Spices—see *Glossary*)
½ teaspoon five spice powder (see Glossary)

200 g (6½ oz) chicken fillet
4 pieces bean curd pastry, 20 cm (8 in) square (see *Glossary*)
1 teaspoon plain flour
vegetable oil, for frying

Dipping Sauce

1 tablespoon chilli paste
1 tablespoon sweet chilli sauce

coriander (cilantro), to serve

- Mix all the dry ingredients together.
- Open up the bean curd pastry with the corner pointed towards you. Spread the onion mixture evenly to the centre of pastry, and then place chicken strips on top.
- Combine the plain flour and 1 teaspoon of water to make a paste.
- Roll up the pastry and seal the edges with the flour paste.
- Heat the oil in a deep fryer (or wok, see ***Basics***) to 180°C (350°F).
- Fry the chicken roll until it floats then drain on paper towels to absorb excess oil.
- Combine the chilli paste and sweet chilli sauce to make the dipping sauce.
- Slice the roll with a sharp knife at an angle and serve with coriander and the dipping sauce.

NOTE

Coriander is an absolute must for this dish as it really enhances the taste.

Bitter Melon Salad

SERVES 4

2 bitter melons
⅓ cup roasted peanuts, chopped
3 tablespoon mayonnaise
2 tablespoon tomato sauce
1 tablespoon sugar

- Mix all sauces and sugar together, return to fridge to chill.
- Cut the bitter melon in half lengthwise, then cut in to bite sizes pieces, then remove the seeds and white pith. Make sure the pith is removed; this can help reduce the level of bitterness.
- Have a bowl of ice water with lots of ice ready for use.
- Bring a pot of water to boil, blanch the bitter melon for 2 seconds, remove and place them in the ice water bowl. Once cooled down, drain well, pat dry with paper towels.
- Sprinkle peanuts on top.
- Serve with sauce on the side or drizzle over the bitter melon.

NOTE

As different brands of mayonnaise and tomato sauce have different levels of sourness and sweetness. The measurements above are just a guide, adjust to taste.

Beef Strips in Sticky Sweet Sauce

SERVES 2 – 4

125 ml (4 fl oz) vegetable oil
25 g (0.9 oz) dry vermicelli noodles/green bean noodles
250 g (8 oz) beef skirt, thinly sliced against the grain
1 teaspoon soy sauce
½ teaspoon sugar
potato flour, a pinch (see *Glossary*)
1 cup corn flour
vegetable oil for frying
½ cup Bloody Plum Sauce
½ teaspoon garlic chilli oil
1 long chilli, thinly sliced at an angle, (deseeded if preferred to minimise the spiciness)

- Heat the wok over high heat, add the oil and fry the noodles until white and crispy.
- Drain them on paper towels and set aside to cool down.
- Marinate the beef with the soy sauce, a drop of water, sugar and potato flour.
- Mix well, then add a teaspoon of oil for a further mix.
- Heat the wok to very hot before adding the oil for frying.
- Coat the beef in corn flour, separate them into pieces and rest for about 30 seconds, shake off excess flour and deep fry the beef strips.
- Fry the beef in batches at 180°C (350°F), once cooked, drain. Cut large pieces (if any) to strips.
- Wait for the oil to heat up again to 180°C (350°F). Return all the beef to double fry the beef to crispy.
- Drain on paper towels, set aside.
- Pour the oil out of the wok, remove any residual particles from frying. In the same wok, add the bloody plum sauce and chilli oil. Turn on the heat to reduce and thicken the sauce, return the beef, toss it quickly to ensure beef is evenly coated with the sauce.
- Serve as is or over crispy noodle.

Stewed Beef Shin

SERVES 4 – 6

2 kg (4 lb) beef shin (heel muscle)
1 tablespoon sesame oil to stir fry

Spices

60 g (2 oz) ginger slices
10 whole cloves garlic, skin on
8 pieces star anise
1 teaspoon Szechuan peppercorns

Stewing Sauces

375 ml (12½ fl oz) soy sauce
1.5 litre (48 fl oz) water
1 tablespoon rice wine
2 tablespoons chilli bean sauce (see *Glossary*)
1 tablespoon sugar
1 shallot (spring onion/scallion)

To serve

1 shallot (spring onion/scallion)
sesame oil, a drizzle
stewed sauces, a drizzle

- Heat up the wok and stir fry the spices with sesame oil until fragrant.
- Wash the beef shin then add to a large pot of water, bring to the boil. Cook for five minutes, then drain and set aside. Rinse pot.
- Return the beef to the rinsed pot, add the stewing sauces and the spices
- Bring to the boil and simmer for about 1½ hours over low heat with the lid on.
- Remove beef from the pot and allow to cool to room temperature, then thinly slice.
- Garnish with shallots and drizzle with some of the stewed sauces and sesame oil when serving.

NOTE

This is a base recipe for several other dishes.

Once cooked, freeze the beef shin and the soup individually.

The stewing stock can be made into soup by adding water.

Depending on the size of the shin, cooking time can vary greatly.
It is ready if you can poke through the shin with a chopstick easily.

This has similar cooking recipe as Traditional Taiwanese Beef Noodle Soup on page 149.

Stewed Beef Shin with Cucumber Salad

SERVES 4

2 beef shins (refer to Stewed Beef Shin recipe on page 84), half lengthwise, then thinly slice
600 g (21 oz) Lebanese cucumber, half lengthwise, then thinly sliced at an angle
2 teaspoons salt
1 long chilli, chopped (deseeded if preferred to minimise the spiciness)
2 garlic cloves, minced
1 tablespoon rice vinegar
1 teaspoon sugar
60 ml (2 fl oz) rice vinegar
sesame oil, drizzle (added just before serving)

- Marinate the cucumber with salt and set aside for 1 minutes. Rinse off the salt and drain well.
- In a large mixing bowl, combine all ingredients and mix well, then place the bowl in the fridge for about 30 minutes, drizzle sesame oil and mix lightly to serve.

NOTE

It is easier to thinly slice the beef shin when it is chilled or in room temperature.

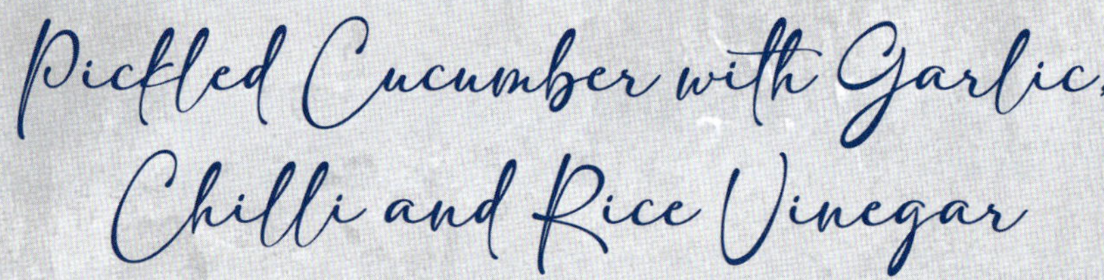

Pickled Cucumber with Garlic, Chilli and Rice Vinegar

SERVES 4

600 g (21 oz) Lebanese cucumber, deseeded and cut into finger size sticks
2 tablespoons salt,
6 cloves garlic, crushed, skin off
1 long chilli, thinly sliced, (deseeded if preferred to minimise the spiciness)
1 teaspoon sugar
60 ml (2 fl oz) rice vinegar
sesame oil, drizzle (added just before serving)

- Marinate the cucumber with salt and set aside for 5 minutes. Rinse off the salt with water and drain well.
- In a large mixing bowl, combine all ingredients and mix well, then place the bowl in the fridge for about 30 minutes, drizzle sesame oil and mix lightly to serve.

NOTE

This refreshing dish can be served on its own or accompanying any rice or noodle dish to give that extra texture to a dish.

Shallot Pancakes

MAKES ABOUT 25 PANCAKES

1 kg (2.2 lb) plain flour
500 ml (17 fl oz) warm water (60°C / 140°F)
½ tablespoon salt
¾ tablespoon vegetable oil
1 cup shallots (spring onion/scallion) finely chopped
vegetable oil for frying

- In a big bowl, sieve through the plain flour then add salt and shallots.
- Add oil into the water, then pour the water oil mixture gradually into the flour mixture while using chopsticks to mix the dough. Do not use processor or hand.
- Cover the dough with a cloth and let it rest in the oven (turned off, no heating) for 30 minutes.
- Gently knead the dough, then divide it into 30-gram pieces. Roll each piece into a small ball.
- Using a rolling pin, flatten each ball into an evenly thin pancake.
- Heat a generous amount of oil in a nonstick pan. Once hot, add a pancake, flip several times until golden.
- Drain on paper towels to remove excess oil.
- Cut into pieces and serve with soy sauce and a drizzle of chilli oil.

NOTE
If made in bulk, separate each pancake with baking paper, then freeze in an airtight container.

Beef Pancakes

SERVES 4 – 6

4 – 6 Shallot Pancakes (see page 89)
1 shallot, julienned, washed and spin dry
1 coriander, chopped
1 stewed beef shin (see page 84)
½ cup beef shin stock
½ cup water
vegetable oil for frying pancake

- Mix ½ cup of beef shin stock with ½ cup of water. Heat up.
- Cut beef shin against the grain in pieces, pull apart, soak in the beef shin and water stock.
- Pan fry the Shallot Pancakes (see page 89).
- Use paper towels to absorb excess oil.
- Place shallot, then pulled beef shin, then coriander on top. Served as is or roll the pastry and use a toothpick to hold the roll together. Cut in half to serve if preferred.

NOTE
Replace beef shin with beef strips (page 83) for crispy texture and different flavour.

Braised Tofu with Ginger and Chilli Sauce

SERVES 4

600 g (21 oz) tofu, cut into triangle shapes
600 ml (20 fl oz) water
125 ml (4 fl oz) soy sauce
2 teaspoons sugar
2 shallots, stemmed
3 cloves garlic, skin on
vegetable oil, for frying
coriander, for garnish

Dipping Sauce

2 tablespoons soy paste
1 teaspoon ginger, minced
1 teaspoon sugar
chilli, if preferred, minced

- Towel dry the tofu to minimise oil spitting.
- In a large pot, combine the water, soy sauce and sugar, and bring the stock to the boil.
- While it is boiling, deep fry the tofu, a few pieces at a time, until golden.
- Once golden, move the tofu pieces into the stock pot.
- Deep fry the shallots and garlic until golden then add into the stock pot with tofu.
- Bring the stock pot back to boil, then simmer for 30 minutes.
- Plate up the tofu with some stock and garnish with coriander.
- Mix dipping sauce together.
- Serve.

String Beans with Fried Garlic

SERVES 1

200 g (7 oz) string beans, cut into 5 cm (2 in) long pieces
1 teaspoon fried garlic, minced
1 teaspoon salt
1 tablespoon chilli, minced, optional (deseeded if preferred to minimise the spiciness)

- In a pot over medium heat, blanch the string beans for about 3 minutes, then remove and drain well.
- In a mixing bowl, combine the string beans, fried garlic, salt and chilli (if preferred), and mix well. Ready to serve.

Fried Garlic Mince

MAKES APPROX ½ CUP

1 cup fresh garlic, peeled and minced, can be done manually or in a food processor.

- Wash the minced garlic and drain as much excess water as possible.
- In a wok on low heat, add some vegetable oil, slowly fry the garlic, stirring constantly to avoid sticking and burning.
- Once cooked and the garlic has turned golden brown, drain quickly.
- The fried garlic can be prepared in bulk and stored in fridge for future use.

NOTE
The washing of the garlic mince is very important.

Large Sharing Plates

Stewed Beef Shin with Chinese Greens

SERVES 4

2 Stewed Beef Shins (see page 84), half lengthwise, then cut in 1 cm pieces
1 cup of beef shin stock
2 bunches of Chinese greens, cleaned and separated
1 tomato, cut into cubes
1 shallot (spring onion, scallion), optional, cut into 2–3 cm (¾–1½ in) pieces
2 teaspoon sugar
2 teaspoon potato flour (see *Glossary*)
Sesame oil, drizzle (added just before serving)

- Combine potato flour with 2 teaspoon of water to make a paste to use later
- In a wok, add the tomato and the beef shin stock together, bring to boil, then put rest of ingredients in. Bring back to the boil, taste it, add more water or sugar if needed to taste. Then simmer for a few minutes
- Add the potato paste and stir well to thicken, then drizzle the sesame oil. Set aside.
- Blanch the Chinese greens, drain well. Place the greens on a plate and spoon the beef and sauce over it.
- Serve.

Pork Belly

SERVES 4 – 6

2.5 kg (5 lb) pork belly, skin on
400 ml (13 fl oz) soy sauce
2 shallots (spring onions/scallions)
5 cloves garlic, with skin off
3–4 pieces star anise
2 tablespoons sugar
½ tablespoon white rock sugar (see *Glossary*)
1 small chilli, whole
coriander (cilantro), to serve

- Clean the pork belly skin with a knife or shaver, then wash pork belly thoroughly.
- Dry well with paper towels or a tea towel. Cut into 4 cm (1½ in) cubes.
- Spread the cubes out on an oven tray and place under the grill to quickly brown all sides.
- Put the pork belly and soy sauce in a large pan over high heat.
- Stir thoroughly until the pork belly absorbs the soy sauce evenly (about 2 minutes).
- Then add enough water to just cover the meat, followed by the shallots, garlic, star anise, sugar and chilli.
- Bring to the boil, then cook over medium heat – slightly higher than simmer, for 40–50 minutes without the lid on and stirring constantly.
- For a softer texture, simmer for an extra 5 minutes, otherwise serve in a bowl and garnish with coriander.
- Remove chilli and shallots before serving.

NOTE
Traditionally, Mum would deep-fry the pork belly until golden, but this also means lots of wasted oil.

Prawns in Jade's Bloody Plum Sauce

SERVES 1 – 2

125 ml (4 fl oz) vegetable oil
25 g (0.9 oz) dry vermicelli noodles/green bean noodles
8 large king prawns (shrimp), peeled and deveined, heads off and tails on
sugar, a pinch
ground white pepper, a pinch
1 tablespoon cornflour
vegetable oil for deep-frying
60 ml (2 fl oz) plum sauce (see *Sauces*)

- Heat the wok over high heat, add the oil and fry the noodles until white and crispy.
- Drain them on paper towels and set aside to cool down.
- Marinate the prawns (shrimp) with the sugar and pepper for a few minutes.
- Coat the prawns in the cornflour, let it rest for a minute.
- Heat the oil in a deep fryer (or wok, see ***Basics***) to 180°C (350°F).
- Fry the prawns in batches, when they float to the surface they're cooked.
- Remove them immediately and drain on paper towels.
- Pour the plum sauce into a lightly oiled wok over high heat to reduce the sauce, then return the prawns to the wok and toss well to coat evenly.
- Serve the prawns on a bed of the deep-fried noodles.

Beef Fillet in Black Pepper Sauce

SERVES 1 – 2

250 g (8 oz) eye fillet, trimmed and cut into bite size pieces

Marinade

a pinch salt
a pinch sugar
1 tablespoon water
½ egg yolk
1 tablespoon potato flour
1 tablespoon vegetable oil

Sauce Mixture

1 tablespoon shallots, finely chopped
1 teaspoon ginger, finely chopped
1 teaspoon white sugar
2 tablespoons soy paste
1 teaspoon steak sauce
1 teaspoon ground black pepper
200 ml (6.7 fl oz) vegetable oil, for frying
mixed leaf salad, to serve

- Combine the eye fillet with salt, sugar, water and egg yolk, mixing well for a few minutes.
- Add in the potato flour and mix well before adding in the vegetable oil and mixing again.
- Heat up the wok over medium heat, add the vegetable oil and when the wok is very hot, add in the eye fillet and stir fry for 1 minute.
- Take the eye fillet out of the work and drain the oil.
- With the same wok, add in all the sauce mixture and stir on a high heat before returning the eye fillet back to the wok and tossing the eye fillet until it is well coated.
- Served on a bed of mixed leaf salad.

Minced Pork Sauce & Soy Eggs

SERVES 10

Minced Pork Sauce

2.5 kg (5½ lb) minced pork
400 ml (14 fl oz) soy sauce
30 g (1 oz) sugar
8 g (¼ oz) rock sugar
1 tablespoon Fried Garlic Mince (see page 94)
1 tablepoon Fried Red Shallots (see page 26)
½ teaspoon ground white pepper
250 ml (8 fl oz) vegetable oil

Soy Egg

10 eggs
1 cup (8.25 oz) soy sauce
2.5 litres (5 pints) water
1 teaspoon cinnamon powder

Minced Pork Sauce

- In a large wok, heat up, add vegetable oil, fry the minced pork to sear in the meat juice in batches. This is the critical step. The searing seals the flavour.
- Put all the fried minced pork into a large pot and add all ingredients, and top up with water to just cover the meat.
- Bring to boil, then simmer for 30 minutes.

Soy Egg

- Place the room temperature eggs in a saucepan of cold water over medium heat. Bring to the boil then gentle simmer for 4 – 8 minutes. Cook the eggs how you would normally cook them, time depends on the size of the egg and amount of water in the pot.
- Once cooked, remove the eggs from the pot and peel.
- Place the cooked eggs in a pot over medium heat with the cinnamon, soy sauce and water. Simmer for 5 minutes. The ratio is 10 parts of water to 1 part of soy sauce.
- Remove pot from heat and allow the egg to cool in the stock for 2 hours.
- Remove the eggs from the pot and marinate in Minced Pork Sauce overnight.
- This will help bring out the flavours in the Soy Egg.

NOTE

This recipe is for bulk quantity. Freeze in portions. Good to use over noodles and rice.

Water Spinach with XO Sauce

SERVE 1 – 2

Tossing Sauce

1 tablespoon XO Sauce (see *Glossary*)
½ teaspoon salt
1 teaspoon sugar
1 small chilli, thinly sliced at an angle
2–3 cloves garlic, sliced

400 g (13 oz) water spinach, cut in 4–5 cm (2 in) pieces
2 tablespoons XO Sauce, to serve

- Combine Tossing Sauce ingredients in a large bowl.
- Boil a pot of water to blanch the water spinach, remove from the pot once the water comes back to the boil. Drain well.
- Combine the spinach with the tossing sauce and mix well.
- Transfer to a plate and top with the remaining XO Sauce.

NOTE
XO Sauce can be purchased ready-made from Asian grocery stores.

Beef in Vinaigrette Yellow Bean Sauce

SERVES 1 – 2

250 g (8 oz) beef skirt, thinly sliced against the grain
¼ teaspoon soy sauce
1 teaspoon sugar
potato flour, a pinch (see *Glossary*)
60 ml (2 fl oz) vegetable oil
125 ml (4 fl oz) ginger, cut into thin strips
2 shallots, cut in 2–3 cm (¾ in) pieces
1 tablespoon yellow bean sauce
½ tablespoon rice vinegar
1 long chilli, chopped (deseeded if preferred to minimise the spiciness)

- Marinate the beef with soy sauce, a drop of water, a pinch of sugar and potato flour.
- Mix well, then add a teaspoon of oil for a further mix.
- Heat the wok to very hot before adding the remaining oil.
- Stir fry the ginger until fragrant and then add the beef and quickly stir fry.
- Once the beef begins to change colour, add the shallot and yellow bean sauce to the wok and stir.
- Finally, add the vinegar and remaining sugar, mix through, remove from the heat.
- Serve.

Taiwanese Sweet and Sour Pork Ribs

SERVE 1 – 2

350 g (11 oz) pork ribs, cut into 4–5 cm (1½–2 in) cubes
1 teaspoon soy sauce
salt, pinch
sugar, pinch
½ egg, lightly beaten
250 g (8 oz) cornflour
vegetable oil, for deep frying
½ onion, cut into strips
2 tablespoons Taiwanese Sweet and Sour Sauce (see *Sauces*)
1 shallot (spring onion, scallion), julienned, washed and spun dry
1 long chilli, to garnish, julienned (deseeded if preferred to minimise the spiciness)
vegetable oil, 1 tablespoon

- Marinate the pork ribs with the salt, sugar and egg for 10 minutes.
- Place the cornflour in a bowl, add the pork ribs and make sure they are well coated.
- Shake off excess flour and leave to rest.
- Heat the oil in a deep fryer (or wok, see ***Basics***) to 180°C (350°F).
- Add the pork ribs a few pieces at a time and deep-fry for 3–4 minutes or until crispy.
- As you remove each batch from the oil, drain them on paper towels.
- Clean the wok, add 1 tablespoon of oil and lightly fry the onion until soft and fragrant.
- Add the Taiwanese Sweet and Sour Sauce and stir constantly to reduce the sauce, return the ribs to the wok and make sure they are well coated. Garnish ribs with shredded shallots and chilli and serve.

NOTE

Taiwanese sweet and sour sauce uses black vinegar which gives a different taste.

Replace pork ribs with lean pork if preferred.

Ginger Shallot Beef

SERVES 1 – 2

250 g (8 oz) beef skirt, thinly sliced against the grain
1 tablespoon soy sauce
½ teaspoon sugar
potato flour, a pinch (see *Glossary*)
60 ml (2 fl oz) vegetable oil
125 g (4 oz) ginger, thinly sliced
6 green shallots (spring onions/scallions), cut in 2–3 cm (¾ in) pieces
1 long chilli, thinly sliced at an angle (deseeded if preferred to minimise the spiciness)

- Marinate the beef with a drop of soy sauce, a drop of water, a pinch of sugar and potato flour.
- Mix well, then add a teaspoon of oil for a further mix.
- Heat the wok to very hot before adding the remaining oil.
- Stir fry the ginger until fragrant and then add the beef and quickly stir fry.
- Once the beef begins to change colour, add the shallots to the wok and stir.
- Finally, add the remaining soy sauce and sugar, mix through, remove from the heat and serve.

Beef in Taiwanese BBQ Sauce with Spinach

SERVES 1 – 2

250 g (8 oz) beef skirt, thinly sliced against the grain
1 teaspoon soy sauce
sugar, pinch
1 teaspoon potato flour (see *Glossary*)
½ tablespoon water
1 tablespoon vegetable oil
1½ tablespoons Taiwanese BBQ sauce (see *Glossary*)
250 g (8 oz) spinach (silverbeet), cut into 5 cm (2 in) strips
2 tablespoons vegetable oil
2 cloves garlic, sliced
1 chilli, thinly sliced at an angle (deseeded if preferred to minimise the spiciness)
½ tablespoon soy sauce

- Marinate the beef with 1 teaspoon of soy sauce, a drop of water, a pinch of sugar and potato flour.
- Mix well, then add the BBQ sauce for a further mix.
- Blanch spinach in water and drain.
- Heat up the wok over high heat, add the oil and stir fry the beef until almost done.
- Add the garlic and chilli to the wok, stir then add in the ½ tablespoon of soy sauce.
- Stir fry until the meat is cooked.
- Place the spinach on a plate and top with the beef to serve.

NOTE

Taiwanese BBQ sauce can be purchased from Asian grocery stores. Spinach can be replaced with other Chinese greens, such as water spinach or Chinese broccoli.

Chicken in Kong-Bao Sauce

SERVES 1 – 2

250 g (8 oz) chicken, cut into 2–3 cm (¾ in) cubes
salt, pinch
sugar, pinch
1 teaspoon potato flour (see *Glossary*)
1 teaspoon vegetable oil
60 ml (2 fl oz) vegetable oil
60 ml (2 oz) ginger
60 g (2 oz) dried chillies
3 green shallots (spring onions/scallions), cut in 2–3 cm (¾ in) pieces
60 ml (2 fl oz) Kong-Bao Sauce (see *Sauces*)

- Marinate the chicken with salt, sugar and potato flour. Once well combined, mix in the oil.
- Heat the wok over high heat then add the oil.
- When the oil is hot, add the chicken and quickly stir fry until cooked.
- Remove from the wok.
- In the same wok, add the ginger and stir fry until fragrant, then add the dried chilli and shallots for a minute.
- Return the chicken to the wok and stir through the Kong-Bao sauce and serve.

Chilli Curry Chicken

SERVE 1 – 2

250 g (8 oz) chicken, cut into 2–3 cm (¾ in) cubes
salt, pinch
sugar, pinch
1 teaspoon potato flour (see *Glossary*)
1 teaspoon vegetable oil

1½ tablespoons curry powder
½ onion, cut into bite-sized pieces
¼ red capsicum (sweet pepper/bell pepper) cut in diamond shape pieces
¼ green capsicum (sweet pepper/bell pepper) cut in diamond shape pieces
3 snow peas
1 chilli, chopped (add more if you like it hot)
¼ teaspoon salt
¾ teaspoon sugar
60 ml (2 fl oz) water
1 teaspoon potato flour (see *Glossary*)
80 ml (2½ fl oz) vegetable oil for stir fry

- Marinate the chicken with salt, sugar and potato flour. Once well combined, mix in the oil.
- Heat the wok over high heat and add the oil. Once hot, stir fry the chicken until cooked, then remove from the wok.
- In the same wok, stir fry the onion until soft and fragrant, then add the curry powder and stir through.
- Toss in the snow peas, capsicum, chilli, salt and sugar for a quick stir fry before pouring in the water.
- Combine the potato flour with 1 teaspoon of water to make a paste.
- Once the sauce comes to the boil, stir in the potato paste to thicken then serve.

Sweet and Sour Chicken

SERVES 1 – 2

Batter
1 cup corn flour
1 cup potato flour
1 tablespoon vegetable oil
1 small egg
1 cup water

250 g (8 oz) chicken, cut into 2–3 cm (¾ in) cubes
salt, pinch
sugar, pinch
1 teaspoon potato flour (see *Glossary*)

1 teaspoon vegetable oil
¼ onion, cut in pieces
¼ red capsicum (sweet pepper/bell pepper) cut in diamond shape pieces
¼ green capsicum (sweet pepper/bell pepper) cut in diamond shape pieces
2 pineapple rings, cut to match the size of the capsicum (optional)
vegetable oil for frying
125 ml (4 fl oz) Sweet and Sour Sauce (see *Sauces*)

- Marinate the chicken with salt, sugar and potato flour. Once well combined, mix in the oil.
- Blend all the batter ingredients together until smooth, can use a blender.
- Transfer the batter to a bowl and add the marinated chicken, ensuring each piece is well coated.
- Heat enough oil to deep-fry the chicken in a wok to 180°C (350°F).
- Carefully place the battered chicken into the hot oil one piece at a time. Fry until golden brown and floating. Remove and drain. If unsure, cut one piece open to check it is cooked through.
- Pour out the used oil and remove any leftover batter bits from the pan.
- Use the same wok on high heat, stir fried onion, red and green capsicums and pineapples briefly, add the sweet and sour sauce, stir well to reduce the sauce.
- Return the fried chicken to the wok and toss quickly to ensure chicken is coated evenly.
- Serve.

Sanbei Chicken with Basil

SERVES 1 – 2

250 g (8 oz) chicken, cut into 2–3 cm (¾ in) cubes
salt, pinch
sugar, pinch
1 teaspoon potato flour (see *Glossary*)
1 teaspoon vegetable oil

60 ml (2 fl oz) sesame oil
60 g (2 oz) ginger, sliced
4 cloves garlic, sliced
2 shallots (spring onions/scallions), cut into 2 cm (¾ in) slices
1 chilli, chopped
2 tablespoons soy sauce
1 tablespoon soy paste (see *Glossary*)
2 tablespoons rice wine
2 tablespoons sugar
125 g (4 oz) basil leaves

- Marinate the chicken with salt, sugar and potato flour. Once well combined, mix in the oil.
- Heat the wok over high heat, add the sesame oil and stir fry the ginger for about 15–20 seconds.
- Add the garlic and chicken to the wok and stir fry until golden. Then add the shallots and chilli for a further stir.
- Add soy sauce, paste, wine and sugar and stir fry until the sauce is reduced. Quickly stir through the basil then transfer to a plate and serve.

NOTE

If you have a cast iron bowl, heat up the bowl on the gas stove or in the oven to produce the sizzling effect when you serve.

Traditionally in Taiwan, Chicken Marylands or whole chickens are used for this dish.

Ginger Shallot Chicken

SERVES 1 – 2

250 g (8 oz) chicken, cut into thin 5 cm (2 in) strips
salt, pinch
sugar, pinch
1 teaspoon potato flour (see *Glossary*)
1 teaspoon vegetable oil
125 g (4.4 oz) ginger, cut into thin strips
6 green shallots (spring onions/scallions), cut in 2–3 cm (¾ in) pieces
½ teaspoon salt
½ teaspoon sugar
1 long chilli, thinly sliced at an angle (deseeded if preferred to minimise the spiciness)
60 ml (2 fl oz) vegetable oil for stir fry

- Marinate the chicken with salt, sugar and potato flour. Once well combined, mix in the oil.
- Heat the wok over high heat before adding the oil.
- Stir fry the ginger until fragrant, then add the chicken and quickly stir fry.
- Once the chicken begins to change colour, add the shallots to the wok and stir.
- Finally, add the salt, sugar and chilli, mix through, remove from heat and serve.

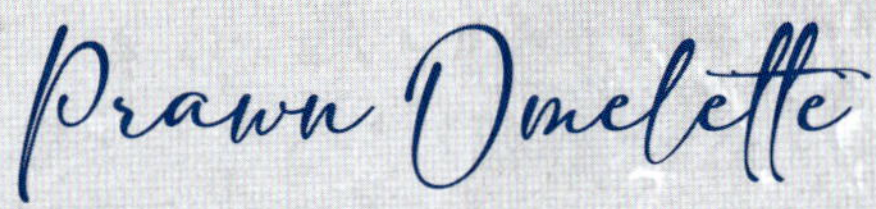

Prawn Omelette

SERVE 1 – 2

8 large prawns (shrimp), peeled and deveined
¼ teaspoon salt
¼ teaspoon sugar
1 pinch white pepper
1 teaspoon cornflour

Omelette mixture

5 large eggs
¼ teaspoon salt
½ teaspoon sugar
1 teaspoon potato flour (see *Glossary*)
2 shallots (spring onions/scallions), finely chopped

125 ml (4.2 fl oz) vegetable oil

- Marinate the prawns (shrimp) with salt, sugar, white pepper and cornflour. Once well combined, mix in 1 tablespoon of the vegetable oil.
- To make the omelette mixture, lightly beat eggs with salt and sugar, set aside.
- Combine the potato flour with 3 teaspoons of water to make a paste and whisk into the omelette mixture.
- Heat the wok over high heat add 80 ml (2.7 fl oz) of oil and stir fry the prawns over high heat for 2–3 minutes, or until they've just changed colour and curled up.
- Add the omelette mixture, stir, then turn the heat back to medium and continue stirring the mixture gently until the eggs are set.
- Pour the remaining oil around the outside edge of the omelette to prevent it sticking, lift the omelette from the edges and slide it onto a plate to serve.

Garlic Prawns with Shallots and Fish Sauce

SERVES 3 – 4

12 large green prawns (shrimp), deveined by cutting open the back but not peeled
10 cloves garlic, finely chopped
2 shallots (spring onions/scallions), finely chopped
250 ml (8 fl oz) vegetable oil
125 ml (4 fl oz) Fish Sauce, heated (see *Sauces*)

- On a plate place the prawns (shrimp) open side up and sprinkle the garlic evenly over the top.
- Start up the steamer, when the water is boiling place the plate of prawns in and steam for about 3 minutes over medium heat. The time will depend on the size of the prawns – as a rule when the prawns turn red, they are almost done.
- Remove the prawns from the steamer, and sprinkle with the shallots.
- Heat up the oil in a wok until almost smoking then pour the oil evenly over the prawns.
- Remove the prawns and place on a clean plate.
- Heat up the fish sauce, pour over the prawns and serve.

Ginger Shallot Prawns

SERVE 1 – 2

8 large prawns (shrimp), peeled and deveined
¼ teaspoon salt
¼ teaspoon sugar
1 pinch white pepper
1 teaspoon cornflour

1 teaspoon potato flour (see *Glossary*)
60 ml (2 fl oz) ginger, sliced
6 shallots (spring onions/scallions), cut into 5 cm (2 in) pieces
¼ red capsicum (sweet pepper/bell pepper), cut into diamond-shaped strips
4 snow peas (mange tout/sugar peas)
4 button mushrooms, cut in half
1 teaspoon sugar
1 teaspoon salt
60 ml (2 fl oz) vegetable oil for stir fry

- Marinate the prawns (shrimp) with salt, sugar, white pepper and cornflour. Once well combined, mix in 1 tablespoon of the vegetable oil.
- Combine the potato flour with 1 teaspoon of water to make a paste.
- Heat the wok over high heat, add the oil and stir fry the ginger until golden.
- Add shallots and prawns to stir until almost cooked.
- Then add all the vegetables and stir fry.
- Mix in the sugar and salt, then stir in the potato paste to thicken the sauce.

Sweet and Sour Fish Fillets

SERVE 1 – 2

250 g (8 oz) white fish fillets, cut in to 2 x 5 x 1 cm (¾ x 2 x ½ in) pieces
salt, pinch
sugar, pinch

Batter
1 cup corn flour
1 cup potato flour
1 tablespoon vegetable oil
1 small egg
1 cup water

vegetable oil, for deep-frying
¼ onion, cut in bite size pieces
¼ red capsicum (sweet pepper/bell pepper) cut in diamond shape pieces
¼ green capsicum (sweet pepper/bell pepper) cut in diamond shape pieces
2 pineapple rings, cut to match the size of the capsicum (optional)
125 ml (4 fl oz) Sweet and Sour Sauce **(see *Sauces*)**

- Marinate fish with the salt and sugar for a few minutes.
- Blend all the batter ingredients together until smooth, can use a blender.
- Transfer the batter to a bowl and add the marinated fish, ensuring each piece is well coated.
- Heat enough oil to deep-fry the fish in a wok to 180°C (350°F).
- Carefully place the battered fish into the hot oil one piece at a time. Fry until golden brown and floating. Remove and drain. If unsure, cut one piece open to check it is cooked through.
- Pour out the used oil and remove any leftover batter bits from the pan.
- Use the same wok on high heat, stir fried onion, red and green capsicums and pineapples briefly, add the sweet and sour sauce, stir well to reduce the sauce.
- Return the fish to the wok and toss quickly to ensure fish is coated evenly.
- Serve.

Pan-Fried Snapper with Ginger, Soy, Chilli and Shallots

SERVES 4 – 6

1 whole 500 g (1 lb) snapper, cleaned
125 ml (4 fl oz) vegetable oil
60 g (2 oz) ginger strips
2 shallots (spring onions/scallions), chopped
1 long chilli, cut at an angle
2 tablespoons soy sauce
1 tablespoon water
1 teaspoon sugar

- Cut 3 slashes into the skin on each side of the snapper.
- Heat the wok over high heat, add the oil and pan-fry the fish until golden brown on both sides.
- Turn the heat to low and continue to cook the fish until tender – it is done if you can easily insert a chopstick into the flesh.
- Push the fish to one side of the wok and stir fry the ginger until fragrant, then toss in the shallots, chilli, soy sauce, water and sugar. Cook for a few seconds.
- Turn the fish to coat it in the sauce.
- Place the fish on a serving plate and pour over the sauce.

Scallops in XO Sauce

SERVE 1 – 2

10 fresh scallops, roe and shell off
sugar, pinch
cornflour, pinch
3 tablespoons vegetable oil
4 cloves garlic, sliced
2 shallots (spring onion/scallion), cut into 2–3 cm (¾ in) strips
1 long chilli, sliced at an angle
a few snow peas (mange tout/sugar peas)
¼ capsicum (sweet pepper/bell pepper) cut into diamond-shaped strips
2 tablespoons XO Sauce (see *Glossary*)
1 teaspoon sugar

- Marinate the scallops with a pinch of sugar and cornflour.
- Combine the potato flour with 1 teaspoon of water to make a paste.
- Heat the wok over high heat, add the oil and then stir fry the scallops until they look plump.
- Remove from the wok.
- In the same wok, stir fry the garlic, shallots and chilli until fragrant, then add the snow peas and capsicums.
- Then add the XO Sauce, sugar and return the scallops to the wok for another stir.
- Serve.

Tofu Stuffed with Minced Pork and Prawn in Black Pepper Sauce

SERVES 2 – 4

10 pieces tofu, cut into 3 x 5 x 1 cm (1½ x 2 x ½ in) pieces
250 ml (8 fl oz) vegetable oil, for deep-frying

Stuffing

250 g (8 oz) minced (ground) pork
60 g (2 oz) minced (ground) prawn
¼ shallot (spring onion/scallion), finely chopped
½ teaspoon Chinese celery, finely chopped (see *Glossary*)
ground white pepper, a pinch
salt, pinch
sugar, pinch

Black Pepper Sauce

125 ml (4 fl oz) soy paste (see *Glossary*)
black pepper, a pinch
½ teaspoon sugar
1 tablespoon water
1 teaspoon sesame oil

10 shallots (spring onions/scallions), green part only
2 teaspoons potato flour (see *Glossary*)

- Combine 2 teaspoon potato flour with 2 teaspoons of water to make potato paste to use later.
- Thoroughly combine the stuffing ingredients.
- Make a hole in the middle of each piece of tofu and fill with the stuffing mixture.
- Pack as much into each one for a tight fit.
- Steam over boiling water for 10 minutes. Let it cool and pat dry with paper towels before deep frying.
- Heat the oil in a deep fryer (or wok, see ***Basics***) to 180°C (350°F).
- Deep-fry the tofu in batches, until crispy on the outside. Drain on paper towels.
- In the wok on medium heat, mix together the Black Pepper Sauce, then add the stuffed tofu.
- Bring the sauce to the boil, reduce the sauce a little, then thicken with the potato paste.
- Serve on hot plate with shallots across to prevent the tofu from sticking on the hot plate.

Soup / Noodles / Congee

Chicken Noodle Soup

SERVE 1 – 2

Soup Toppings

1–2 stalks Chinese celery, finely chopped (see *Glossary*)
1 shallot, finely chopped
1 teaspoon salt
2 drops soy sauce
1 teaspoon sugar
pinch ground white pepper
½ tablespoon Fried Red Shallots (see page 26)

500 ml (8 fl oz) water (or chicken stock if available)
250 g (8 oz) chicken, cut into strips
100 g (3½ oz) dry noodles or 200 g (7 oz) fresh noodles
Chinese greens
coriander (cilantro) to garnish

- Follow the instructions on the noodle packaging to cook the noodles, then use the same pot to blanch the Chinese greens.
- Drain until ready to use.
- In another pot, bring water/stock to the boil and put the chicken strips in for a few minutes until cooked.
- Place the noodles in a bowl, top with the remaining ingredients and pour in the chicken and stock/water. The heat will release the flavours.
- Garnish with coriander.

NOTE

If Chinese celery is not available, use Western celery which is less aromatic.

Mum always keeps trimmed excess chicken pieces (not presentable enough for stir fries) to make chicken stock. Bring water to the boil, add the chicken pieces and simmer for 10 minutes.

Noodles with Minced Pork Sauce in Chicken Stock

SERVE 1 – 2

Soup Toppings

1–2 stalks Chinese celery, finely chopped (see *Glossary*)
1 shallot, finely chopped
1 teaspoon salt
1 teaspoon sugar
ground white pepper, a pinch
½ tablespoon Fried Red Shallots (see page 26)

500 ml (16 fl oz) water or Chicken stock if available
100 g (3½ oz) dry noodles or 200 g (7 oz fresh noodles)
Chinese greens
3 tablespoons Minced Pork Sauce (see page 107)

- Follow the instructions on the noodle packaging to cook the noodles, then use the same pot to blanch the Chinese greens.
- Drain well and place noodles and Chinese greens in a serving bowl.
- Add the Chinese celery, shallot, salt, sugar, pepper, and fried shallots into the soup.
- In another pot, bring water or chicken stock to boil, and pour over the noodles and ingredients. The heat will release all the flavours.
- Pour the Minced Pork Sauce on top and garnish coriander to serve.

NOTE

Chicken stock can be made using leftover chicken trimmings or bones.
Simply reduce the stock, pour it into an ice cube tray, and freeze.
For each serving of noodle soup, add a frozen stock cube for a flavour boost.

Cold Noodle Salad

SERVES 2

Sauce Mixture

2 tablespoons sesame paste
1 tablespoon soy sauce
1 tablespoon sesame oil
1 tablespoon sugar
1 tablespoon black vinegar
2 teaspoons wasabi (optional)
50 ml (2 fl oz) warm water
500 g (8 oz) cooked egg noodles
½ cucumber, julienned
½ carrots, julienned
1 egg, whipped, cook on a flat pan then julienned
1 cup cabbage, thinly julienned

- Mix all sauces together, then add warm water gradually while stirring. Adjust the amount of warm water used, depends on the sesame paste purchased. The consistence should be sticky and thick. Set sauce aside in fridge.
- Follow the instruction on the noodle packaging to cook the noodles. Once cooked, quickly blanch in ice cold water, drain well and place in the fridge.
- Prepare the vegetables, set aside.
- Put the noodles in a bowl, place vegetables on top, drizzle the sauces over then serve.
- Toss the noodles and vegetable and sauces well prior to consuming.

NOTE

The thickness of the sauce and how well the noodles are drained will significantly affect the flavour. Too much water can dilute the taste, so make sure the noodles are well-drained, and the sauce is thick and concentrated. If it is too dry, you can always add a bit of water.

Stir-Fried Noodles with Chicken and Vegetables

SERVES 2 – 4

250 g (½ lb) chicken, thinly sliced
2 shallots, cut in inch long, separate white and green parts
500 g (8 oz) cooked noodles
100 g (3½ oz) carrots, cut in thin strips
½ onion, thinly sliced
2 cups Chinese greens (stemmed) or cabbages (thinly sliced)
3 tablespoons vegetable oil
1 tablespoon soy sauce
1 teaspoon sugar
1 tablespoon black vinegar
sesame oil, drizzle (optional)

- In a large pot, blanch the noodles and then blanch the carrots, drain well and set aside separately.
- Heat up a wok, then add oil. Once oil is hot, stir fried the chicken for 1–2 minutes. Once cooked, take the chicken out. Set aside.
- With the same wok, add onion and stir till soften, add carrots and white part of the shallots for another stir. Then add the noodles and vegetables, stir.
- Return the chicken, add soy sauce and black vinegar and sugar to the wok, stir until all mixed.
- Final step, add the green part of shallots and sesame oil for a final mix, then serve.

NOTE

Depends on the vegetables chosen, cabbage can be hard which may require a quick blanch to help the cooking speed. The aroma of stir fried noodles comes from the soy sauce and vinegar. You may substitute the vegetables to your liking, the principle is whatever takes longer to cook, add it in first.

Traditional Taiwanese Beef Noodle Soup

SERVES 2 – 4

2 kg (4 lb) beef shin (heel muscle)
1 tablespoon sesame oil to stir fry

Spices

60 g (2 oz) ginger slices
10 whole cloves garlic, skin on
8 pieces star anise
1 teaspoon Szechuan peppercorns

Stewing Sauces

2 tablespoons chilli bean sauce (see *Glossary*)
2 tablespoons sugar
2 shallots (spring onion/scallion)
3.75 litre (8 pint) water
750 ml (25 fl oz) soy sauce

To serve

500 g (16 oz) cooked white noodles
sesame oil, to drizzle
1 shallot (spring onion, scallion), finely chopped
1 stalk coriander (cilantro), chopped
a few stalks Chinese greens, chilli oil to taste (optional – see *Glossary*)

- Heat up the wok and stir fry the spices with sesame oil until fragrant.
- Wash the beef shin then add to a large pot of water, bring to the boil. Cook for 5 minutes, then drain and set aside. Rinse pot.
- Return the beef to the rinsed pot, add the stewing sauces and the spices.
- Bring to the boil and simmer for about 1½ hours over low heat with the lid on.
- Remove beef and set aside. Sieve the liquid for the soup and reserve.
- Follow the instructions on the noodle packaging to cook the noodles, then use the same pot to blanch the Chinese greens.
- Place the noodles, Chinese greens and a few pieces of cut beef shin in a bowl, and pour over enough soup to cover. The soup itself may be too salty as it varies on the stewing process. Add water to taste.
- Drizzle with sesame oil, garnish with shallots and coriander or chilli oil to serve.

NOTE

This recipe is perfect for making in bulk. Depends on the size of the shin, cooking time can vary greatly. If you can poke through the shin with a chopstick easily, it is ready. Once cooked, slice the beef shins into 2 cm (½ in) thick pieces. Freeze the beef along with the soup in individual serving portions. This makes your next meal a breeze – just cook the noodles, heat up the beef and soup, and you are ready to serve!

Chicken Congee

SERVES 2 – 4

250 g (8 oz) rice
2.25 litres (5 pints) water, can mix with some chicken stock
ginger, a few slices, thinly julienned
250 g (8 oz) chicken, thinly sliced

Seasoning

1 teaspoon salt
1 teaspoon bonito powder (see *Glossary*)
ground white pepper, a pinch
2 shallots (spring onions/scallions), finely chopped
1 stick celery, finely chopped (or Chinese celery if available – see *Glossary*)

- Wash rice well and drain.
- In a large pot, bring rice and water to the boil, stirring constantly to avoid the rice from sticking to the pot. Once the water is boiled, turn the heat down to a simmer and cook the rice without a lid.
- Meanwhile, use another pot of boiling water to blanch the chicken quickly. Drain.
- Once the rice is cooked to the desired texture, and the water is significantly reduced, add the chicken and seasoning and bring back to the boil. Remove the pot from the heat.
- Add the shallots and celery to the congee, mix well and serve.

NOTE
This recipe gives you a softer texture than a regular risotto. If you prefer to have your congee almost soup-like, add more hot water before adding the chicken.

Chinese Turnip Congee

SERVES 4

Turnip Mixture

250 g (8 oz) rice
2 tablespoons dried shrimp
3.75 litre (8 pint) water
60 ml (2 fl oz) vegetable oil
150 g (5 oz) pork, minced (ground)
50 g (2 oz) Chinese turnip, finely chopped

Seasoning

1 teaspoon salt
1 teaspoon bonito powder (see *Glossary*)
ground white pepper, a pinch
2 shallots (spring onions/scallions), finely chopped
1 stick celery, finely chopped

- Wash rice well and drain.
- Soften the shrimp in water then drain.
- In a large pot, bring rice and water to the boil, stirring constantly to avoid the rice from sticking to the pot. Once the water is boiled, turn the heat down to simmer and cook the rice without a lid.
- While the rice is cooking, heat the wok over high heat then add the oil, stir-fry the pork, turnip, shrimp and seasoning until fragrant.
- Once the rice is cooked to desired texture, add the turnip mixture and bring back to the boil. Remove the pot from the heat.
- Add the shallots and celery to the congee, mix through well and serve.

Dry Toss Minced Pork Noodle with Soy Egg

SERVES 2

Dry Toss Sauce

1 shallot, finely chopped
100 g (3½ oz) dry noodles or 200 g (7 oz) fresh noodles
1 tablespoon soy paste
1 teaspoon Fried Garlic Mince (see page 94)
½ tablespoon Fried Red Shallots (see page 26)
1 teaspoon sugar
sesame oil, drizzle

Chinese greens
3 tablespoons Minced Pork Sauce & 1 Soy Egg (see page 107)

- Follow the instructions on the noodle packaging to cook the noodles, then use the same pot to blanch the Chinese greens.
- Drain the noodles well and place in a mixing bowl, add all dry toss sauce ingredients and mix really well.
- Place noodles in a bowl and pour the Minced Pork Sauce over the top.
- Serve with Chinese greens and Soy Egg.

Rice Ball Soup

SERVES 6

500 g (16 oz) glutinous flour
400 ml (13½ fl oz) water
300 g (10 oz) pork loin, diced
2 tablespoons vegetable oil for stir fry
1 cup shiitake mushrooms
1 tablespoon dried prawns (shrimp)
1 teaspoon ground white pepper
1 cup chives, chopped
3 tablespoons Fried Red Shallots (see page 26)

- Mix the flour and water together (it will be on the dry side like a scone mixture).
- Make one small patty from about 1/10th of the mix and drop this into boiling water.
- When it floats and expands, take it out of the water and return it to the remaining flour and water mix.
- Knead the patty back into the mix.
- The water it absorbed during cooking will be enough to moisten all the flour.
- Once the cooked and raw dough are well mixed, add in the vegetable oil for further kneading.
- Knead well then roll and flatten and cut into long strips then to small pieces to roll into tiny balls (like marble balls).
- Soak the mushrooms in water until soft, squeeze out the water, thinly slice the mushrooms, save the water to use later.
- Soak the dried prawns (shrimp) in water, then drain well.
- Heat up a wok, add oil and stir fry the pork loin. When almost cooked, add mushrooms and prawns for another quick stir, season with pepper and add the mushroom water back in with the soy sauce. Once boiled, set aside.
- Boil water in a big pot, then add the rice balls to boil for 4–6 minutes (depends on the size of the balls, they are ready when floating for a minute).
- In a big serving bowl, place cooked rice balls, add the pork mixture, chives and Fried Red Shallots. Then pour some of the water used to cook the rice balls over the chives to make soup.
- The pouring of hot water over the chives cooks the chives and releases more flavour.

Beef, Tofu and Vegetables Soup

SERVES 2

150 g (5 oz) beef, diced
3 teaspoons potato flour (for marinading)
50 g (2 oz) carrots diced, blanched and drained
50 g (2 oz) celery, diced
50 g (2 oz) water chestnuts (can be canned), diced
50 g (2 oz) mushrooms, diced

150 g (5 oz) tofu, cut into cubes

3 cups water
1 egg whites
2 teaspoon potato flour (for thickening)
1 teaspoon salt
½ teaspoon ground white pepper

- Marinate the beef with 1 tablespoon of water, a pinch of salt and pepper and 3 teaspoons of potato flour, mix well and set aside
- Boil the water, add all vegetable ingredients except tofu and bring the pot to boil.
- Add marinated beef and tofu for another quick boil and season with salt and pepper.
- Bring the pot to the boil again, then turn the heat down. Mix 2 teaspoons of water with the potato flour to make paste, add to the soup gradually, stir to thicken.
- Beat the egg whites, then stir the soup in circular motions while pouring the egg whites slowly to the soup.
- Turn off the heat right away.
- Serve.

NOTE
This soup is light. It will require a little bit more salt if serving over rice or noodles.

Rice

Taiwan Rice is ∞.

Rice

Taiwanese Rice is shiny, distinct grains with aroma and springy texture. It has a tasty fragrance but also diverse flavours, textures and characteristics.

A major crop in Taiwan, the rice fields account for about 20% of the farming land area, mainly located in Taichung City, Changhua County, Yunlin County, Chiayi County, Tainan City and Hualien County. According to the rice qualities, rice in Taiwan is divided into three major categories: japonica, indica and glutinous rice.

The japonica rice is also called 'Pon-Lai Rice', which has short, round and transparent grains with sticky, soft and springy texture when cooked. The indica rice has long, narrow and also transparent grains, and it can be further divided into hard indica rice that has hard, foamy and dried texture and soft indica rice with soft texture. Generally, hard indica rice is mainly used as the raw material for processed food. On the other hand, soft indica rice has a texture similar to japonica rice when cooked and perfect for direct consumption. The glutinous rice has opaque grains and is especially soft and very sticky when cooked. Glutinous rice can be divided into two kinds, one is short-grain glutinous rice and the other is long-grain glutinous rice. The former is suitable for making sweet rice diets like rice wine and 'tangyuan' (glutinous rice dumpling). The latter is suitable for making savoury rice diets like 'zongzi' (sticky rice dumpling), rice cake and steamed glutinous rice. Rice in Taiwan has diverse varieties which meet different needs and is people's must-have staple food for daily life.

Information above from Taiwan's Ministry of Agriculture.

Sticky Rice with Pork and Mushroom

MAKES ENOUGH FOR A PARTY OF 20

50 g (1.7 oz) dry shiitake mushrooms
30 g (0.1 oz) dried prawns (shrimp)
50 g (1.7 oz) Fried Red Shallots (see page 26)
1 kg (35 oz) glutinous rice
½ kg (17 oz) pork loins diced
2 teaspoons white pepper
2 teaspoons sugar
80 ml (2.7 fl oz) soy sauce
60 ml (2 fl oz) vegetable oil
sweet chilli paste
½ cup chilli paste, ½ cup sweet chilli sauce, mix well together
coriander (cilantro) to serve

- After soaking the glutinous rice for 4 hours, drain the water and spread the rice over cheesecloth. Place in a steamer and steam for 40 minutes.
- Soak the dried mushrooms in warm water until soft. Squeeze out the excess water, thinly slice the mushrooms, and reserve 1 cup of the soaking liquid for later.
- Soak the dried shrimp in warm water to rehydrate, then drain well.
- While the rice is steaming, heat a wok over medium-high heat. Add oil and stir fry the pork loin until almost cooked. Add the mushrooms and shrimp, stir fry briefly, then season with white pepper. Pour in the reserved mushroom water, sugar and soy sauce. Bring to a boil, then set aside.
- Place the steamed glutinous rice in a large bowl. Pour the pork mixture, Fried Red Shallots over the rice and use a spatula to quickly mix everything until the rice is evenly coated.
- Serve with sweet chilli paste and fresh coriander on the side.

NOTE

It is very important to mix rice well while it is very hot, the heat helps absorb the flavours into the rice, continues the cooking process. Depends on the time needed to prepare the pork mixture, time it right, so the pork mixture is ready when the rice is steamed.

Chicken Fried Rice

SERVES 2 – 4

150 g (5 oz) chicken breasts, cut into thin 5 cm (2 in) strips
½ teaspoon salt
½ teaspoon sugar
1 teaspoon cornflour
2 tablespoons vegetable oil
500 g (16 oz) steamed rice
2 eggs
¼ medium onion, diced
¼ medium carrot, diced and cooked
60 g (2 oz) diced shallot (spring onion/scallion), green end only
½ tablespoon soy sauce
ground white pepper, a pinch

- To marinate the chicken, mix with a pinch of salt, sugar, cornflour, and some vegetable oil.
- Leave for 10 minutes.
- Heat the wok to almost smoking, add some oil to moisten the wok, then add the eggs.
- Stir fry the eggs and scramble into pieces. Remove them from the wok when well done.
- Use the same wok to stir fry the chicken. When the chicken is almost cooked, add onions and carrots for a quick stir, then add the rice. Mix all together until the rice is heated through, then return the egg back to the wok.
- Sprinkle the remaining salt, sugar and pepper over the rice and stir.
- Drizzle with soy sauce and add chopped shallots for a final stir.

NOTE

Add ingredients to your liking, fried rice is all about what is available in the fridge. The most important part of the process is heating the wok before cooking. This will improve the texture of the fried eggs and the rice. The green end of shallots add colour to the fried rice.

Bacon Fried Rice

SERVES 2 – 4

150 g (5 oz) bacon, cut into pieces
¼ teaspoon salt
½ teaspoon sugar
2 tablespoons vegetable oil
500 g (16 oz) steamed rice
2 eggs
¼ medium onion, diced
¼ medium carrot, diced and cooked
60 g (2 oz) diced shallot (spring onion/scallion), green end only
½ tablespoon soy sauce
ground white pepper, a pinch

- Heat the wok to almost smoking, add some oil to moisten the wok, then add the eggs.
- Stir fry the eggs and scramble into pieces. Remove them from the wok when well done.
- Use the same wok to stir fry the bacon. When bacon is cooked, add onions and carrots for a quick stir, then add the rice. Mix all together until the rice is heated through, then return the eggs back to the wok.
- Sprinkle the remaining salt, sugar and pepper over the rice and stir.
- Drizzle with soy sauce and add chopped shallots for a final stir.

NOTE

Add ingredients to your liking, fried rice is all about what is available in the fridge. Bacon tends to be salty, hence the salt is reduced in this recipe. The most important part of the process is heating the wok before cooking. This will improve the texture of the fried eggs and the rice. The green end of shallots add colour to the fried rice.

Prawn Fried Rice

SERVES 2 – 4

8 large prawns (shrimp), cleaned and deveined
½ teaspoon salt
½ teaspoon sugar
1 teaspoon cornflour
2 tablespoons vegetable oil
500 g (16 oz) steamed rice
2 eggs
¼ medium onion, diced
¼ medium carrot, diced and cooked
60 g (2 oz) diced shallot (spring onion/scallion), green end only
½ tablespoon soy sauce
ground white pepper, a pinch

- To marinate the prawns (shrimp), mix with a pinch of salt, sugar, cornflour, and some vegetable oil.
- Leave for 10 minutes.
- Heat the wok to almost smoking, add some oil to moisten the wok, then add the eggs.
- Stir fry the eggs and scrambled into pieces. Remove them from the wok when well done.
- Use the same wok to stir fry the prawns. When the prawns are almost cooked, add onions and carrots for a quick stir, then add the rice. Mix all together until the rice is heated through, then return the egg back to the wok.
- Sprinkle the remaining salt, sugar and pepper over the rice and stir.
- Drizzle with soy sauce and add chopped shallots for a final stir.

NOTE

Add ingredients to your liking, fried rice is all about what is available in the fridge. The most important part of the process is heating the wok before cooking. This will improve the texture of the fried eggs and the rice. The green end of shallots add colour to the fried rice.

Desserts

Sticky Rice with Wolfberries and Sultanas served with Sweet Peanut Powder

MAKES 6

peanut powder and coriander
500 g (16 oz) sticky rice
2 tablespoons sugar
2 tablespoons Chinese wolfberries (see *Glossary*)
2 tablespoons sultanas
4 tablespoons sweet peanut powder (see *Glossary*)
1 stalk coriander (cilantro), chopped

- Soak the rice for 4 hours, then drain.
- Place the rice in a steamer and poke holes through it with a chopstick to allow the steam to get through.
- Steam for 30 minutes.
- When cooked, place in a bowl and stir in the sugar.
- Mix the wolfberries and sultanas together.
- Line 6 small bowls with cling film.
- Place a spoon of the wolfberries and sultana mix in the bottom of each bowl and pack the rice in over the top – fill it well so it takes on the shape of the bowl.
- Invert each bowl onto a serving plate. Sprinkle the sweet peanut powder and chopped coriander around the dessert and serve.

NOTE
This dessert is served warm or hot.

Mochi with Brown Sugar Syrup, Crushed Peanuts and Black Sesame

MAKES ENOUGH FOR A PARTY

500 g (16 oz) glutinous flour
400 ml (13½ fl oz) water
2 tablespoons vegetable oil
½ cup peanuts, crushed

Sugar Syrup
500 ml (16 fl oz) water
300 g (10 oz) white sugar
100 g (3 oz) raw sugar
ginger, a few slices

- Mix the flour and water together (it will be on the dry side like a scone mixture).
- Make one small patty from about 1/10th of the mix and drop this into boiling water.
- When it floats and expands, take it out of the water and return it to the remaining flour and water mix.
- Knead the patty back into the mix.
- The water absorbed during cooking will be enough to moisten all the flour.
- Once the cooked and raw dough are well mixed, add in the vegetable oil for further kneading.
- Knead well, cut the dough into equal size pieces around 50 g (1.6 oz), then roll and flatten into 5 cm (2 in) diameter raw mochis.
- Drop them into boiling water in batches, cook for 6 minutes before removing from the water and drain.

Sugar Syrup

- Combine the water, white sugar, raw sugar and ginger in a pot and leave to boil. Stir occasionally.
- Once the ingredients have dissolved, the sugar syrup is ready to use.
- Place mochi on a plate, drizzle over the sugar syrup, sprinkle with some crushed peanuts and black sesame to serve.

NOTE

Raw mochi can be kept in the freezer in airtight containers.
Leftover sugar syrup can be refrigerated and kept for another use.

Sweet Red Bean with Vanilla Ice Cream

MAKES ENOUGH FOR A PARTY

500 g (1 lb) red beans
375 g (13 oz) sugar or to taste
80 g (3 oz) potato flour mixed with 60 ml (2 fl oz) water to make a paste
vanilla ice cream, to serve
cocoa powder, to serve

- Soak the red beans overnight to soften them.
- The next day, bring them to the boil in about 2.5 litres (5 pints) of water.
- Reduce the heat to very low and simmer for about 90 minutes or until the beans are soft.
- Be careful not to cook them too fast or they will break apart or lose their skins.
- Add the sugar to the pot and then the potato paste, which will soak up any remaining liquid and thicken the red beans. Chill in fridge.
- Serve a scoop of red bean with ice cream and dust with cocoa powder.

NOTE

Any cooked red beans that are left over can be frozen for future use. It can also be used to make red bean soup. Just add hot water and sugar to taste.

Sticky Rice Cakes in Ginger Syrup with Sweet Peanut Powder

MAKES ENOUGH FOR A PARTY

½ kg (1 lb) glutinous rice flour
400 ml (13½ fl oz) water
500 g (16 oz) sugar
250 ml (8 fl oz) water
1 piece ginger
sweet peanut powder (see *Glossary*), to serve

- Thinly slice the ginger and wash the slices. This preserves a good colour.
- Boil the ginger, sugar and water until sugar dissolves.
- Mix the flour and water together (it will be on the dry side similar to a scone mixture). Make one small patty from about 1/10th of the mix and drop this into boiling water. When it floats and expands, take it out of the water and return it to the remaining flour and water mix.
- Knead the patty back into the mix. The water it absorbed during cooking will be enough to moisten all the flour.
- Knead well then roll and flatten into patties about 2 cm–3½ cm (¾–1½ in) in diameter. At this point the cakes can be frozen.
- Drop them into boiling water in batches, cook for 6 minutes before removing from the water and draining.
- Place the cakes on a plate, pour over the ginger syrup and add a few ginger slices. Top each rice cake with the sweet peanut powder and serve.

Glossary

OF UNUSUAL INGREDIENTS

Most ingredients listed below and throughout this book should be available in Asian grocery stores. Specific brands used in this book are named here and with photo in p 30.

Bai-Chao (Hundred Spices): A combination of different herbs and spices. Frequently used in marinating, preserving, grilling and deep-frying. Generally, very expensive and available in Chinese herbal stores.

Bean Curd Pastry: Is generally gluten free and made from yellow beans. Look for the thinnest pastry possible to give a much nicer texture when deep-frying.

Black Vinegar: Made from rice with fermented fruits and vegetables. Suitable for soups and noodles. Specific brand: Kong Yen.

Bonito Flakes: Made from smoked bonito fish. They look like wood shavings. Commonly used in Japanese cooking.

Bonito Powder: A flavour enhancer made from smoked bonito fish.

Chilli Oil: Available ready-made in most Asian grocery stores.

Chilli Bean Sauce: Made from fermented soy beans with chilli and garlic. Widely used in Asian cooking and generally, very salty.

Chinese Celery: Thinner and more fragrant than Western celery, the stems are longer and hollow. It is often mistaken for coriander and perfect for soups.

Chinese Wolfberries: Are orange-red, dried sultana-shaped Chinese herbs, also known as goji berries. Available in Chinese herbal stores and some Asian grocery stores.

Dumpling Pastry Wrappers: These wrappers are round and made from plain flour. Available from the refrigerator section in most Asian grocery stores.

Five Spice Powder: Available in Chinese herbal stores and Asian grocery stores. Quality varies according to herb and spices grading.

Fried Shallots: Made from small red Asian shallots. An essential topping ingredient in non-soy sauce based soups.

Glutinous Rice Flour: Frequently used in Asian desserts to give more texture.

Potato Flour: A much better thickening agent, which gives a clearer and glossier finish than cornflour.

Preserved Chinese Plums: Are a popular Chinese snack food and available in powder also. Salty, sour and acidic in flavour.

Rice Vinegar: It should be made in a rice wine fermentation process, generally is made from rice. Specific brand: Kong Yen.

Rice Wine: Made from Japonica rice, popular with women post postpartum confinement meal preparation.

Soy Paste: Much thicker than soy sauce. Not as strong in flavour as oyster sauce. Suitable for vegetarians. Specific brand: Kim Lan.

Soy Sauce: Made from fermented soy bean pastes. Specific brand: Kim Ve Wong.

Spring Roll Pastry Wrappers: Thin, elastic-like wheat-based wrappers. Small, medium and large sizes are available from the refrigerator section in most Asian grocery stores.

Sweet Peanut Powder: Ground roasted peanuts mixed with castor sugar. The ratio is generally 2:1.

Sweet Potato Flour: Also known as tapioca powder. It gives a much crunchier taste when deep-fried. Preferred in Taiwanese cooking and comes in a crumbed variety.

Szechuan Peppercorns: Look similar to black peppercorns and originally from Szechuan province in China. They give a much stronger aroma and flavour.

Taiwanese BBQ Sauce: Main ingredients include soybean oil, fish, garlic, spices, shallots, sesame oil, dried shrimp and chilli. Specific brand: Bull Head.

White Rock Sugar: Are lumps of sugar which give food a cleaner taste. There is also a yellow-coloured variety available.

Wonton Pastry Wrappers: These thin, square wrappers are made from plain flour. They are available from the refrigerator section in most Asian grocery stores.

XO Sauce: Originated in Hong Kong in the 1980s. Main ingredients include dried scallops, dried shrimp and salted ham.

Yellow Chives: These are part of the Chinese chive family and have a lighter flavour. Generally, not widely available.

Index

First published in 2025 by New Holland Publishers

newhollandpublishers.com

A record of this book is held at the National Library of Australia.

ISBN 9781760794620

Managing Director: Fiona Schultz
General Manager/Publisher: Olga Dementiev
Designer: Andrew Davies
Proofreader: Tiffany Zehnal
Photography: Joe Filshie, Sue Stubbs, Maria Michael, Max Kennedy and Max Huebscher
Food Styling: Georgie Dolling, Carolyn Fienburg
Production Director: Arlene Gippert

Keep up with New Holland Publishers:

NewHollandPublishers
@newhollandpublishers